Nick Pye and **Justin Wright** firs innovation project for a world lead a consultant and Justin the client. F shortcomings in the worlds of innov they set up Mangrove. Since then, ι.., ιιave set up five further companies and worked on over 500 innovation and growth projects for some of the world's biggest business and brands. They both hold non-exec roles in fast growth start-ups.

After leaving Oxford University, Nick worked for strategy and marketing consultancies, as well as for a Virgin backed start-up linked to Oxford University. With Mangrove he has explored his interests in the links between strategy, risk and behaviour, and led numerous projects in markets as diverse as Nigeria, Russia, Kuwait, Pakistan and the USA.

Justin began his career as an FX trader before going on to study psychology and entering the corporate world. After a number of innovation roles in specialist units at P&G and Diageo, he became board director for a consumer trends and research agency and then set up Mangrove with Nick. With a particular interest in the field of human performance, he has led numerous global projects in categories as diverse as drinks, financial services and agriscience.

They share an interest and passion for how the principles of growth and 'STRETCH' that lead to sustainable success can be applied to individuals and teams across business, sport, and beyond, and why some ventures in these fields succeed while others fail. The result is *Stretchonomics*.

STRETCHONOMICS

Nick Pye & Justin Wright

SILVERTAIL BOOKS • *London*

First published by Silvertail Books in 2018
www.silvertailbooks.com
Copyright © Nick Pye and Justin Wright 2015
1
The right of Nick Pye and Justin Wright
to be identified as the author
of this work has been asserted in accordance
with the Copyright, Design and Patents Act 1988
A catalogue record of this book is available
from the British Library
978-1-909269-32-3

CONTENTS

PREFACE

We live in an age of benchmarking. It's now almost impossible to resist the temptation to compare ourselves and our lives with those of others – whether they be friends, neighbours, work colleagues or celebrities. This can be an unhealthy and sometimes disheartening distraction from the graft of daily life, largely because it is often impossible to understand how happy those around you *really* are. The outward appearance of success doesn't necessarily equate to internal fulfilment.

What's more, when we look at those lucky buggers who seem more successful than us – those people who appear capable of achieving anything they set their minds to – we can have no real understanding of what drives this ability to get more from life, or what they have done to get to where they are. Is it hard work, luck, commitment, risk-taking, charm or some secret ingredient that we don't have? Damn their eyes! They're probably up to something shady – probably illegal – and their silver-lined bubble will burst eventually. The sooner the better...

Years ago, we lunched with a very rich but wonderfully unassuming man who advised us to avoid comparing ourselves with others because 'there's always someone richer, slimmer or better-looking than you.' We assumed this was him sharing a general maxim rather than making a comment on us specifically, so took on board his advice! However, on a professional level, we have a long-held fascination with the differences between success and failure. Since 2005, our day job has involved helping some of the world's largest companies and best-known brands find ways to grow by thinking and acting differently. Some people call this innovation – although we find this an increasingly limiting word. Regardless of what you call it, it's a challenging job and a discipline in which failure is the norm rather than the exception. Very few businesses manage to achieve or exceed their goals, and only one in ten new products can be considered a long-term success. According to recent Bloomberg research, 80% of new businesses fail, and being able to systematically deliver success is becoming a rare phenomenon. So trying to better understand why some companies achieve significant and sustainable growth while others under-deliver has become the core focus of our work.

Over the years we realised that no matter how different our clients and their ambitions were, the same few questions were coming up over and over again:

- **Why do some teams within businesses find it easier to grow than others?**
- **Why are some businesses successful while others aren't?**
- **What is it that sets the success stories apart from the strugglers?**
- **Is it down to individuals, the organisations around them, or is it both?**

We were seeing these questions, or variations of them, time after time, but the differences between the clients, whether it was sector, geography, size, or ambition, meant that the answers appeared to be as varied as the people we were giving them to. So we dug deeper. We did some proper research. We looked at statistics, the backgrounds of key people, the cultures of these businesses, how quickly they made decisions, how fast they had grown and wanted to grow, how employees were rewarded, how their leaders led, how targets were set, how mistakes were dealt with, and so on. We even looked beyond business to the world of elite sport to understand if the same drivers of success applied to top level athletes and sports teams.

And that was when we started noticing patterns. Regardless of where they were, who they were or what their business or discipline was, there were deep and important similarities between successful people in any walk of life. And just as significantly, unsuccessful people and unsuccessful businesses had plenty in common too.

Understanding these patterns – which we will explain fully in the coming pages – enabled us to create STRETCHONOMICS, a framework for making ambitions a reality. STRETCHONOMICS is based on a combination of the rigour and resource management of economics, the opportunity spotting and original thinking of innovation, and the psychology of individual performance and motivation. We believe success for individuals or companies comes from understanding those things and harnessing them for your own purposes. We believe the principles outlined here are as relevant to someone who wants to run a marathon as they are to someone trying to double the turnover of a multinational corporation.

*

STRETCHONOMICS begins with the concept of STRETCH. To 'stretch' is to reach that little bit further than might feel comfortable. Stretching is what happens when we look at our current situation and ask: what's *next*? STRETCH – the concept – shows how anyone can find the right balance between their ambition and their commitment, define their goals and then work towards them in a manageable, achievable way. This, we found, is a core driver of success. It's what the hobbyist runner does when she decides to run her first marathon, what the amateur guitarist does when he decides he's going to perform in public for the first time, what the start-up company and huge corporation do when they decide to launch a new product or enter a new market. Learning to stretch is about developing and maintaining the ability to grow in a way which matches your expectations and goals: real, achievable growth. We found in our research that those who enjoyed more success had aligned what they wanted with what they were prepared to do to get it.

There are other theories of success and performance out there. We should know – we've devoured them all. The problem? Almost all are one-dimensional. They posit that exceptional results are primarily driven by singular characteristics – whether that's how 'gritty' we are, or how many hours of practise we're prepared to put into a single endeavour. These theories and books are often wildly successful. That's because their simplicity is memorable. They appeal to our very human temptation to think that, if we could just change *one* thing, we might suddenly achieve great success. But a decade and more of running a successful innovation agency – and our professional and personal interest in what makes teams and individuals succeed – have convinced us that the reality is very different. In STRETCHONOMICS we believe that achievement is the output of a more complex formula, with seven distinct components which we will explore in this book.

Failing to address any of these seven dimensions compromises the chances of reaching the stretching ambition you have for yourself. Seven dimensions of success might seem a lot to tackle, but there are seven days in the week, seven colours of the rainbow, and somehow we seem to navigate these things without any problem. In this book, we'll dissect how and why each factor contributes to the formula for success, as well as providing guidance for how to improve your odds of a positive outcome. You'll have to read on to find out more. In the meantime, they can be boiled down to two key questions:

What do I want?
and:
What am I prepared to do to get it?

STRETCHONOMICS will show you how to answer them in a way which suits you and is tailored to your personal circumstance.

STRETCHONOMICS is an holistic system. No one element is more important than the rest – and, while reading this book from first page to last may seem most natural, don't be afraid of dipping in and out of each of our seven STRETCH dimensions along the way. And if, like us, you've a thousand things to do and there aren't enough hours in the day, that's OK too. We've designed this book so that even the time-starved can begin their STRETCH challenges fully-armed. By reading the Introduction, the Conclusion, and the handy summaries at the end of each chapter, we're confident that you'll begin to understand the concepts at the core of our thinking.

Armed with STRETCHONOMICS principles, you will be able to interrogate any situation and, by doing so, build a plan to unlock your own personal growth. We have worked this concept through with some of the world's biggest companies, entrepreneurs, professional sports teams, military professionals – and, more painfully, applied it to our own work, with both our clients and our own start-up businesses. That's how we know it works. STRETCHONOMICS can make a difference, regardless of who you are and what you're trying to achieve. It may also help you better understand those friends or neighbours who seem to be getting more out of life than you. Whether you choose to emulate them is entirely up to you – but it's nice to have the choice, right?

Nick & Justin
Soho, London.

INTRODUCING **THE STRETCH ZONE**

- Exploring the Stretch Zone
- Aligning ambition and commitment
- Lining up the Seven Dimensions of STRETCH

Why do some people seem capable of achieving anything they set their minds to while others fall short of their goals? Why do some sports teams achieve consistently high performances while others only manage to raise their game occasionally? Why do some companies achieve significant and sustainable growth whilst others never live up to their high expectations?

Decades of creating step-change growth for some of the world's biggest companies and best-known brands has led us to one answer that we believe works for all of us, whether in a business, sports or personal context: those who experience sustained success are able to consistently match their ambitions with their commitment. Or, to put it another way, are our lofty ambitions matched with the necessary resources, skills, mind-set and behaviours to achieve them? If so, the chances of successful growth are increased – but, if not, we are more likely to experience the disappointment of unmet expectations or be left ruing missed opportunities. It may sound simple, but the reality, in our experience, is that the two are often out of kilter.

When our ambition is balanced with our commitment, we enter and embrace life in the Stretch Zone – a place where we're constantly challenged, where growth is always on the horizon, and where we define our success by how fulfilled we are on a deep, personal level. STRETCHONOMICS is the art and science of the

Stretch Zone itself: getting us there, keeping us there, and providing us with the foundations of solid and sustainable growth.

Life in the Stretch Zone is always exhilarating, sometimes uncomfortable and rarely easy. To get there, individuals and organisations need to develop the ability to stretch – to set and align appropriate goals, resources, behaviours and mind-sets. In STRETCHONOMICS there is no silver bullet, no one-size-fits-all approach to success. Life doesn't work like that, and nor does business. We can't promise a magical elixir to automatically transform you or your organisation's fortunes, but what we can promise is that, over the next seven chapters, we'll drill down into each of the seven dimensions of STRETCH, arming you with the tools and knowledge to embark upon successful STRETCH journeys of your own. And the first step to locating and entering your own Stretch Zone is to understand the place where most of us, whether we're businesses or individuals, ordinarily reside. Welcome to… the Comfort Zone.

The Comfort Zone

As human beings, we all have a natural tendency to live life in what's come to be known as the 'Comfort Zone', a place of contentment, happiness and security. And why not? Wikipedia (which appears to be becoming the Oxford English Dictionary of our age) defines this place as a 'psychological state in which a person feels familiar, at ease, in control, and experiences low anxiety.' With your family and friends, this is lovely. After all, who doesn't want to feel 'at ease' with the people closest to them? Who doesn't want to live a life free of stress and not subject to the usual anxieties of life?

Yet, in personal and business development, being in the Comfort Zone is not always ideal. Sure, you might be content and safe in your Comfort Zone, but you're also 'limited' and your achievements will only ever be 'steady'. A person operating in their Comfort Zone might never open the door to a new and rewarding relationship. Similarly, a business operating in its Comfort Zone would lack ambition, plod along with low (or no) growth and little, if any, commitment to change anything for the better. In the worst-case scenario, a business operating in the Comfort Zone might find itself blind to the prevailing trends of the outside world; it might miss significant opportunities or, worse still, be so committed to its sedate life cycle that, eventually, the demand for its services moves on and its core business collapses. Consider the example of Noland Bushnell, the founder of computing giant Atari. From 1970 to 1976, Bushnell – then running one of the world's pioneering computing firms – employed a bright young man who, on deciding to set up on his own, offered Bushnell a third of his new company. All this young man wanted in return was an investment of $50,000. Bushnell turned him down for what probably seemed, at the time, to be good reasons. Except that the young man's name was Steve Jobs and his new company was to be called Apple Computers, soon to be the first company to be valued globally at more than a trillion dollars.

Or consider Kodak, once the world's leading brand in cameras and other photography equipment. Kodak invented the digital camera long before you might expect, building the world's first in 1975 – but, fearing that it would impact sales of their core products and services, they suppressed it. Fast forward to 2013, the year when digital cameras ruled the world; that same year, Kodak only escaped bankruptcy by selling its patents for $525 million. Neither of these companies had seen the value in reaching beyond. The gravitational pull of their own Comfort Zones, the temptation of sticking to the known, living in the world of incremental improvement and not 'rocking the boat', had been too much, and soon they were eclipsed by something bigger and more ambitious coming in their wake.

The origins of the term 'Comfort Zone' lie in an experiment carried out in 1908 by two psychologists, Robert M. Yerkes and John D. Dodson, who were interested in how performance is affected by anxiety levels. They concluded that too little anxiety (which they called the 'Comfort Zone') produces weak performances, and that too much anxiety (which they called the 'Danger Zone') does exactly the same. For Yerkes and Dodson, there was a zone between the two, a zone where just the right amount of anxiety could be the catalyst for optimal performance – whether that be on the sports' field, in the boardroom, or in just about any other walk of life. What Yerkes and Dodson had hit upon was a place that, many years later, we would come to know as the 'Stretch Zone', a place between the extremes where opportunities – for life, for growth, for expansion – reside. In the Stretch Zone you're being challenged just enough to engage you, to keep you thinking, to keep you hunting for opportunities and new ways of doing things; while, at the same time, you're not being compelled to reach for the unobtainable.

The difference between the Comfort and Stretch Zones is at the start of any STRETCH journey, but it's important to understand that neither is a place with fixed boundaries. Rather, both are dynamic, with boundaries that shift and change. What is stretching for us now might become comfortable in the future, once we have acquired new techniques, behaviours and mind-sets. In the world of physical fitness they call this a 'body plateau'. Anybody familiar with life in the gym will be aware of the way that, at the start of a new regime, results can come quickly. In those first stages, when you're pushing your body to do things it has not done before, the immediate results can be encouraging – but there comes a point at which the same old routine no longer yields the same results. Why? Well, your body has reached a 'plateau'; what once stretched it, has now become comfortable. And the same is true in business. Companies that once entered their Stretch Zone often find that, unless they keep progressing, things become stale again; what was once the Stretch Zone has become the Comfort Zone, with all the dangers that that entails. We were once told that, if a great white shark stops swimming, it will sink and drown. By swimming, sharks force water into the gills, where they can extract oxygen from it. Put simply: if they stop swimming, they die. We can't think of a more fitting metaphor for the concept of STRETCH: it's progress that keeps us alive.

It's easy to see the appeal of the Comfort Zone – and in fact it has a physiological effect on our bodies that it is difficult to deny. When we're in a familiar situation, we feel good because our brain is releasing 'happy hormones' like dopamine and serotonin. On the flip side, when we're fearful and stressed, our body releases chemicals like adrenaline, the fight or flight hormone, which heightens our senses, increases our heart rate, and generally prepares us for action. If you stop and think of it physiologically, then, it's clear why so many of us stay in our Comfort Zones for so long. Why wouldn't we, when we feel happy and safe – and all that's out there, in the zones beyond, is anxiety and stress?

And yet, to stay in the Comfort Zone presents challenges of its own, and chief among these is the risk of complacency – or even atrophy. Remember that gym-goer who found herself at a body plateau? Well, if she were to stop training altogether, her body wouldn't retain the flexibility and strength she's worked hard to achieve. When we stop using our muscles, they atrophy; everything we've worked hard to develop wastes away with disuse. The same is true of our mental function – if we stop using our brains, pretty soon we don't have the ability to do so – and in business the same holds true. Unless we're constantly being challenged – to put it bluntly, unless we remain in the Stretch Zone – we run the risk of the skills fading away.

Complacency is a killer and nobody knows this more than the former telecoms giant Nokia. In 2003, the Finnish firm was synonymous with mobile phone technology. Nokia were at the forefront of the mobile revolution. They pioneered predictive text, developed the first mobile video games – remember *Snake*? – and tech enthusiasts slavered over the new Nokia in a way that nobody had seen before. Nokia made the mobile phone not just a communication device, but a valuable commodity. It seemed that nobody could challenge their global dominance.

That is, of course, until 2007, when the first iPhone arrived and transformed not only the mobile phone market, but also the way many of us communicate with each other and the wider world. At that point, Nokia utterly dominated the nascent smartphone market, with a market share of almost 50%. The following year, that had tumbled to 43%, then 41%, then 34% – until, in 2013, it hit a new low of only 3%. The catastrophic decline of the mobile giant could not have been more dramatic – and, on reflection, its directors put it down to one word: complacency. Nokia bestrode the mobile world like a colossus. It had innovated, it had set the golden standards, it had built and energised a market – and it had not thought, for a second, that it could be challenged. Complacency had slipped in. They started believing that, because they ruled the world now, they would rule it forever. In the meantime, pretenders to the throne had been making innovations of their own, and it took only a few years for Apple to have displaced Nokia as the world's premier smartphone giant. In Stretchonomics terms: Nokia had not committed to staying ahead, and had slipped unknowingly into a Comfort Zone of their own. By the time they realised it, it was too late, and, in 2013, they were forced to sell out to Microsoft, effectively surrendering Nokia as a brand.

Could Nokia have done anything to avoid its fate? Well, ironically, they were no strangers to change. Nokia began life in 1865 as a ground wood pulp mill in southern Finland and, across the generations, made several significant changes and mergers, until they finally came to telecommunications in the mid-20th century. The rise and fall of Nokia is not unique. Across the history of business there are examples of companies where failure to keep moving has led to calamity, while the refusal to sit still has led to the greatest reward. In 2000, Netflix was battling to stay alive. Its then core business – selling DVDs by mail order to a small number of customers – no longer looked viable, and so they decided to embrace the rapid expansion of broadband technology and stream their movies to online subscribers instead. The change of direction would be a costly affair and, with their current business in dire straits, they were in no position to finance the progression themselves. So they decided to approach the giant of their sector, Blockbuster Video Entertainment Inc, offering them the entire business for $50 million. Blockbuster turned the offer down flat – why would the dominant company in the film and game rental business need to buy a company like Netflix for that amount? Well, the rest is history: seven years later, when the internet had made even more advances, Netflix was booming and Blockbuster in deep trouble. Blockbuster came into the streaming market, which Netflix was by now dominating, far too late. In 2010, Blockbuster posted a loss of $1.1 billion and was worth little more than $24 million, while Netflix was worth $13 billion. Three years later, the very last Blockbuster Video store closed down.

The difference between the two companies? Well, Blockbuster Video had remained in its comfort zone for too long, refusing to accept the necessity to adapt or die until it was too late. Netflix, meanwhile, had embraced change. They had stepped out of their comfort zone. They had, to put it simply, *stretched.*

Life In The Stretch Zone

Remember Yerkes and Dodson? Their principle of 'optimal anxiety' is the key to understanding Stretch. By inducing an anxiety response in mice, Yerkes and Dodson came to the conclusion that, up to a certain level, anxiety is a catalyst to greater performance. After that, when we're put under too much stress, our performance deteriorates rapidly. The psychologist Daniel Pink calls this 'productive discomfort'. 'Like Goldilocks,' he says, 'we can't be too hot or too cold.'[1.]

The Stretch Zone, then, is a place where we can actually harness our anxieties, a place where the stresses we naturally face can be converted to positives and spur us on to solid, long-term growth. In the Comfort Zone, we seek to avoid failure, while in the Stretch Zone we look to actively improve. In the Comfort Zone, we might be complacent while, in the Stretch Zone, we're hungry; in the Comfort Zone, we avoid conflict, while in the Stretch Zone we confront our challenges head on. The trick is to consistently locate ourselves on the Yerkes-Dodson curve, where we have *just enough* anxiety to propel us onward, but not enough to paralyse us.

What is life like in the Stretch Zone? Well, think back to 2016, the year Leicester City pulled off the unthinkable feat of winning the English Premier League. The club's first top-flight championship in their 132-year history was sealed with two games left to play. Leicester went from being 5000/1 outsiders to champions. The pioneer of this success was the team's quietly-spoken manager, Claudio Ranieri. Ranieri had far fewer resources at his disposal than his wealthier rivals, and a playing squad that lacked depth and star names. Yet somehow he was able to create a powerful team spirit, employ daring counter-attacking tactics, and get the very best out of his players through a combination of sports science and the science of motivation. The combination of all these factors turned City into a winning team – but what is perhaps most impressive is how Ranieri managed to keep his team performing at their peak for the duration of the season. In Stretchonomics terms, he was not only able to get his team into the Stretch Zone – but to keep them there for thirty-eight league matches. He'd successfully aligned the ambitions of the club, team and supporters with the resources the club and team were willing and able to commit.

Or look to the story of Laura Penhaul. We first met Laura in 2013. A physiotherapist by training, Laura was seeking sponsorship for an upcoming challenge. Her goal? Well, Laura had never been the sort of person to shirk a challenge, and this time she had decided she was going to take a four woman team and row across the Pacific Ocean.

This got our attention.

At 34 years old, Laura had forged a successful career working with marathon runners, skiers and Paralympians, helping them to achieve incredible goals. The way she described it to us, Laura had a special tool in her arsenal, one which set her apart. In order to give each of her clients the best possible treatment, Laura sought to gain a deeper understanding of the demands of what they do by undertaking a challenge in their specific fields. When she was treating her first marathon runner, she ran her first marathon. When she was working alongside professional skiers, she taught herself how to ski. Laura saw her work as a process of constant challenge and adjustment. She was constantly setting herself a new bar.

Which is why, when she first took up the challenge of working with a Paralympian athlete, she had to stop and think. What challenge could she possibly find that would compare with the experience of being, for instance, an amputee? Laura quickly came to the realisation that there was no experience in the world that could recreate the kind of life-changing experience many Para-lympians had been through. To gain the kind of insight she felt that she needed, she instead resolved to find a challenge that would 'get as close as possible to understanding what it is that you draw on when you're faced with something so hard you want to give up but have no choice in the matter – you just can't.' For Laura, this new challenge had to be immense, mentally and physically relentless.

Eventually, Laura decided that she would cross the Pacific Ocean, the world's largest ocean which, at 64 million square miles, covers one third of our planet. The journey she chose, from California to Australia, was 8,446 miles long and, she discovered, had never been done as a continuous three-stage row. Success would mean setting two world records. Even better, Laura had never rowed before. She wasn't even a sailor. Everything was different and everything was unknown. She had found her significant adversary.

Not for the first time, Laura Penhaul had stepped into her own personal Stretch Zone.

And do you know what? She did it. Four years after laying herself the challenge, Laura and her team of three other female rowers set off. The trip was intended to last six months but, in the end, it took nine – all thanks to El Nino's capricious temperament. The first leg took them from Santa Barbara to Hawaii and lasted 68 days. After seven days restocking the boat and provisions, they covered the second leg from Hawaii to Samoa in 97 days. There followed another week of rest before they embarked upon the journey's final leg: Samoa to Cairns in Australia, a journey of 77 days. Rowing days – a total of 242 – were two hours on, two hours off, 24 hours a day, every day. Think about that for a minute: rowing two hours on, two hours off, for 242 out of a total of 256 days. The physical and mental strength required to get through that is astonishing.

And yet... success hadn't always been guaranteed. By the time Laura and her crew were out on the ocean, they used their magnificent mental reserves to push through, but at the outset – some four years previously – failure was very much in their minds. Right up until the team were embarking for the first time, failure seemed much more likely than success. It might seem natural that the hardest part of the challenge was the nine months at sea – but, in her own self-deprecating way, Laura says that the rowing was the easy part. The four years it took to get the boat in the water compelled Laura to become an expert in fundraising, team selection and dynamics, to learn about electronics and boat maintenance, and so much more. This, rather than the physical feat, was where she needed to stretch the most.

Laura was only able to complete her formidable challenge because she has always understood the power of living in the Stretch Zone. Her story is an extraordinary one. She has proven herself, time and again, to be an extraordinary woman. But the Stretch Zone is not just accessible to the extraordinary among us. And nor is Stretchonomics. Whatever your Pacific Ocean is, whether to launch a new business, or just to finally be able to swim the length of your local swimming pool, the value of the Stretch Zone is limitless. Living here is invigorating, energising, filled with life lessons and things we can learn about ourselves. The sense of constantly bettering ourselves, always trying new things and garnering new experiences might even, according to some researchers, be one of the secrets of lasting happiness – and, in the 21st Century, we need it more than ever.

And that's the mind-set behind Stretchonomics: the belief that taking the conscious effort to keep growing makes us more productive, and therefore happier, in the long term. Living in the Stretch Zone demands a combination of ambition, hunger, resourcing, capability and courage, and the capacity to look carefully at ourselves and make some robust decisions – but it might just be exactly what you need to help you become more fulfilled. Because, after the many and varied clients we've worked with over the past decade, one thing is abundantly clear: always moving forwards, never sliding back, makes human beings – *us* – happier and more productive in the long term. This is life in the Stretch Zone in its purest, most unfiltered form.

How To Find The Stretch Zone

The Comfort Zone doesn't have to be the enemy. There are times when reverting to comfort is exactly what we need. A marathon runner cannot return to the start of the race directly after completing the last one, and a business that has just been through a period of rapid expansion will often need to catch its breath, take stock and allow things to settle before embarking on a new stretch of its own. A successful career is often marked by rapid acceleration followed by periods of consolidation. In an increasingly frenetic and interconnected world, relaxation matters. When we use the Comfort Zone to decompress, it can be a positive influence on our lives. But when we become institutionalised in the Comfort Zone, we're missing out on opportunities for growth. Businesses begin to act as if there is greater risk in innovating than in doing nothing, which leaves them open to attack from smaller, hungrier 'challenger' brands, while individuals shut themselves down to the chances for new and fulfilling relationships, experiences and achievements.

Yet venturing out of the Comfort Zone doesn't, by definition, mean you'll end up in the Stretch Zone. It's a wilderness out there! So how exactly do we know where the Stretch Zone is? Now that we've acknowledged the dangers of remaining too long in the familiar, how do we know exactly what kind of *different* is right for us?

In the coming chapters we'll be exploring the seven dimensions of Stretchonomics, but for now let's think of them in two broad areas. We consider your 'ambition' to be defined by your S and your T – your SCOPE and TARGET – and your 'commitment' to be defined by your R, E, T, C, and H, your RESOURCES, EXECUTION, TECHNIQUE, COURAGE and HUNGER. When our ambitions (what we *want* to do) are perfectly aligned with our commitments (what we have to do to get there), we have entered the Stretch Zone.

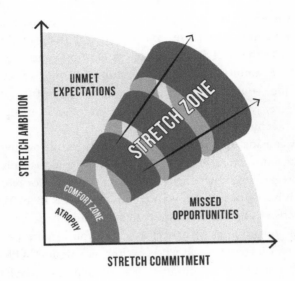

If you think this means that you have to emulate Laura Penhaul or Leicester City and look to achieve the near impossible, look back at the chart and think again. The Stretch Zone is a big place. More particularly, it's personal to you. Laura Penhaul had huge ambition and huge commitment. Her ambition matched her commitment, and this put her in the very heart of her own Stretch Zone. But what if she'd had huge ambition and no commitment? She'd have languished somewhere beyond the Stretch Zone. And if she'd had no ambition and huge commitment? Well, she'd have languished somewhere outside the confines of the Stretch Zone again.

The Stretch Zone isn't about doing everything at 110%; it's about aligning our ambition and our commitment and keeping them in balance, at a particular point in time. It exists only where our ambitions and our commitments are in synch, providing us with the perfect landscape in which to develop and grow.

Still not sure how to find your Stretch Zone? Imagine you're an amateur cyclist, training for your first competition. Your ambition is big – you want to come top three in the race, first time of trying. But your commitment doesn't match your ambition: you don't, or won't, make the time for training. Try plotting yourself on our chart. A big ambition and a low commitment means that you'd have to plot yourself somewhere beyond the line of the Stretch Zone. Here, your chances hitting your target and feeling good about any achievement are tiny.

Now consider that you're competing in the same cycling race, but your ambition is limited – all you want to do is finish the course, regardless of whether it takes you two hours or ten. Your ambition is low, but what if your commitment was high? What if you practised and practised and practised for the occasion, if you invested your savings in first class kit, if you hired a personal trainer to drill you in the very best cycling techniques? With a low ambition but a high commitment, you might easily complete the challenge you've set yourself – but are you really *stretching* yourself? We'd argue not. Instead, you've bypassed the Stretch Zone altogether.

Perhaps you're beginning to see the relationship between our ambitions and our commitments? Only when they're perfectly aligned are we truly stretching. Whether our ambitions are vast or modest, only when our commitments match them are we truly stretching.

Stepping out of the Comfort Zone is only a minor part of the Stretchonomics equation. In fact, most of our work in innovation is concerned with helping clients who either have the ambition to step out of the Comfort Zone, but haven't matched that with their commitment; or who are heavily resourced, full of capability, but lack the necessary drive to grow.

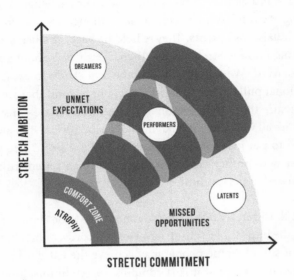

Outside the Stretch Zone, there are two common danger zones. In Stretchonomics, we think of those companies and individuals with high growth ambitions but little sense of what they need to invest – in terms of money, emotion, original thinking and more – to deliver them as **Dreamers**. We often see this with companies who have just acquired a new leadership team and instantly feel they need to declare an heroic ambition: to be the market leader, to double the business inside five years – and all without being aware of what they need to commit in order to get there. In Stretch terms, they might have defined their Stretch Ambition – but they haven't considered what their true commitment is and what their resources, techniques and behaviour will be. This leads to unmet expectations.

Some of the multi-nationals we work with are challenged in exactly this way, but there are others who have an abundance of resource, capability and tenacity, but no real sense of direction. These companies have amazing assets but can't figure out why they're not growing as fast as their competitors, and their challenge is one of ambition. We think of these companies – though they could easily be individuals – as **Latents**. They're holding back, or stuck in a rut.

Getting into the Stretch Zone, then, clearly isn't about a single stride forward. We might need to take that stride to escape the gravitational pull of the Comfort Zone, but beyond that we need to make sure that our ambition and commitment are constantly aligned. It's all well and good having bold aspirations – but are you prepared to put in what is necessary to make it work? Are you a **Dreamer** with unmet expectations, or are you a **Latent** ruing so many missed opportunities?

Being in the Stretch Zone, then, does not have to be about accomplishing the impossible, setting new world records, or breaking the barrier of sound. Some people may achieve the extraordinary in their Stretch Zones, but it isn't compulsory. Ambitious growth is not better than modest growth; in fact, both are terms that can only really be defined in relation to what your own situation is. Twenty press-ups a day might be a perfectly sensible stretch goal for somebody who has only just decided to get fitter, or has limited time and motivation – but it might not be so sensible for an Olympic athlete. In last season's Premier League, Watford FC and their new manager Walter Mazzarri set themselves a target: they would reach 17th place in the league and, by doing so, survive until the next season. What might have been a modest goal to a more accomplished and consistent side still demanded significant commitment and effort for Mazzarri and his players. What wouldn't have stretched Manchester United, certainly stretched Watford. And what was the result? Well, they did it. They finished 17th and lived to play another day – and all because their ambition and commitment were perfectly aligned.

In Stretch, then, all is relative. Stretching isn't about making us all superhuman or creating world-dominating businesses. It's about giving us the tools to be good enough to achieve what it is that we want – and what will ultimately fulfil us.

The Seven Dimensions of Stretch

The seven dimensions of Stretchonomics help to navigate the Stretch Zone. They're not only about escaping the gravitational pull of the Comfort Zone, but about keeping you and your organisations in tune so that you don't stray above the line, into that place where ambition outweighs commitment – or fall below, into that place where our capabilities are vast but our ambitions too slight. Stretchonomics is based on a combination of the rigour and resource management of economics, the opportunity spotting and original thinking of innovation, and the psychology of individual performances and motivation. It offers a framework for making ambitions real.

And here's how it works – the seven key factors that together help us navigate our way into the Stretch Zone:

Imagine, for a moment, that the time has come for you to enter the Stretch Zone – not as a company, but as an individual. Your goal is to run a marathon, something the imaginary you has always wanted to do. We know what our Stretch challenge is – but now let's break it down in Stretchonomics terms and examine what we need to do to get, and stay, in the Stretch Zone.

The first thing a marathon runner must do is articulate his or her Stretch Ambition by drilling down and defining their SCOPE and TARGET. In Stretchonomics, SCOPE is the act of defining our growth challenge, while TARGET lays out a specific and appropriate goal to achieve. For our marathon runner, settling on SCOPE is as simple as deciding what event they're going to run and where. Should this be a full marathon? A half-marathon? Or even something more ambitious – the infamous Marathon des Sables, six days of running through the blistering heat of the Sahara desert? With SCOPE in mind, our marathon runner must then decide on his or her TARGET – or, in this case, *how quickly am I going to finish the race*? Finding an appropriate stretch goal is critical to entering the Stretch Zone. Should we run the race in a competitive four hours, or at a more leisurely six? What is the right goal for me, in my own situation? Our TARGET sets our expectations and, in combination with SCOPE, creates our Stretch ambition. Too stretching a TARGET leads to unrealistic expectations – how can a beginner runner hope to win their very first marathon? – while too modest a target fails to push you out of the Comfort Zone. Could our marathon runner, for instance, really consider it a stretch to complete their run across the breadth of an entire day?

With our marathon runner's Stretch ambition now defined, they must turn to examining their Stretch commitments. They know what they're going to do. Now they must articulate what they're willing to do in order to get there. What RESOURCES does our marathon runner have at hand to help them achieve their ambition? Is there time enough in their schedule to allow for training? Do they have the ability, financial and otherwise, to free up that time, or to buy the equipment they might need to train? As we'll see in the coming chapters, the availability of what you need to achieve your goals is of vital importance – all resources are finite, but most are stretchable. If there isn't enough time in the day to train, is running a marathon really a realistic proposition – or might our SCOPE and TARGET need to be revised?

The marathon runner must also consider his or her EXECUTION. What training plan must they put in place? What nutritional choices can they make to ensure they're running at peak capacity? And how can they understand, along the way, exactly *how* they're doing? As we'll see, our ideas grow through action – it isn't enough to sit down and theorize about marathon running; we need to get out there and see what works in practice. How can we combine original thinking with action, to get the best out of ourselves along the way?

What TECHNIQUES do we have to best prepare us for the race? How does a marathon runner develop the necessary physical and mental skills to complete their Stretch challenge? The 'flair myth' exposed by writers like Malcolm Gladwell and Matthew Syed shows that you cannot rely on raw talent alone – so how does our marathon runner know that they have the right pacing, the right breathing, to make it through a race? What works for one race might not work for another – the demands on the body of a long-distance runner are vastly different to sprinters, for instance – so our TECHNIQUE is necessarily driven by the choices we've made with our SCOPE and TARGET. Might one or both need rethinking to line up correctly with what techniques we adopt?

Attempting to run a marathon for the first time will not be easy, and it will make big demands of the mental abilities of our runner as well. Success will require COURAGE in the face of adversity – not just to take the plunge and commit to the race, but to get through the setbacks they'll undoubtedly face along the way. How do we develop the necessary fortitude to deal with discomfort and risk? When your training plan is interrupted by a minor injury, do you give up and go home, or do you find another way to train until you are fully fit? When you wake in the morning to complete a 10km training run before work, only to find it cold and wet and windy outside, do you roll over and put it off until tomorrow – or do you grit your teeth, get out there and do it?

The final Stretch dimension our marathon runner has to consider is their HUNGER. When we've fulfilled our ambition, how ready are we to pick ourselves up, dust ourselves off, and sign up for another marathon further down the road? Do we keep on stretching, or do we fall back permanently into our own Comfort Zones?

The world of professional sport is littered with examples of people who have missed opportunities or failed to fulfil their potential. In the world of football alone there are too many to mention – Denilson, Ronaldinho, Gascoigne, Owen: all talented players who didn't deliver on the promise they showed early in their careers. And a Gallup poll of 2015 returned a startling parallel in the world of businesses: that, on average, companies could achieve 59% more growth in revenue per employee, purely by helping them to fulfil their whole potential.[2]

The Australian tennis player Nick Kyrgios is a crystal-clear example of what can happen when we have all the talent and resources in the world, but lack a rigorously defined SCOPE and TARGET – and, perhaps, don't have the HUNGER to succeed. Kyrgios was a prodigy, winning the boys championship at the 2013 Australia Open, reaching the quarter finals at Wimbledon in 2014, even beating Rafael Nadal – then the world No. 1 – *en route*. By June 2016, Kyrgios was ranked 18th in the world but, after he was defeated by Andy Murray at Wimbledon that same year, questions began to be asked about his future in tennis. A quick Stretchonomics diagnosis of Kyrgios and his career shows why. Kyrgios did not lack the Resources to support his career; nor did he lack the Techniques and Execution to succeed at the highest level – in fact, he had the talent to be among the top 5 players in the world. But what Kyrgios did lack was structure – he didn't even have a coach – and ambition. Kyrgios had previously stated that he wanted to get better at tennis, but that he wasn't actually in love with the sport – he was just good at it. Accordingly, his Stretch ambition wasn't there: his SCOPE and TARGET were lacking, and this impacted negatively on other Stretch dimensions like COURAGE and HUNGER. His lack of ambition could be seen in how he'd relaxed playing video games on the morning of his big game against Andy Murray, or how he spent time before one of his own significant matches spectating another match. To get properly in the Stretch Zone, Kyrgios would first have to define his SCOPE and TARGET more effectively – not just to get better, but to win Wimbledon, to be the World No 1 – and then start fine-tuning his other Stretch dimensions so that everything was aligned. Or, to put it even more baldly than that, Kyrgios first needed to decide: is tennis what he really *wants*?

At the very heart of Stretchonomics is the idea that it takes only one of these dimensions to be overlooked or to become misaligned for us to fall out of the Stretch Zone. If our marathon runner doesn't have the Courage to get through setbacks, if he doesn't have the Resources of enough time to train, if his Target is too ambitious or his Hunger too small, the chances of successfully completing the race become significantly reduced.

But our marathon runner is just one of manifold examples of Stretchonomics in practice. What's of particular interest to us is how the underlying principles of Stretch can be applied to help individuals, teams, businesses and other organisations grow in a successful, sustained and fulfilling way. In each chapter of this book, we'll explore in detail one of the seven dimensions of Stretch, why they're important and how they work in concert with one another to align Stretch ambitions and Stretch commitments. Through examples from the worlds of sport, business and everyday life, we'll provide food for thought and guidelines for how to improve your chances of success. Each dimension will be illustrated with a mixture of engaging case studies, scientific theory and thought-provoking personal anecdotes from our own experiences of stretching our clients and ourselves. And, by the end of this book, it's our hope that you'll be provisioned with the right tools and knowledge to diagnose your own stretch challenges, get your dimensions aligned, and embark upon a period of strong and sustainable growth.

SO, IN SUMMARY...

Before we embark on our exploration of the Seven Dimensions of Stretchonomics, keep in mind the course we're about to steer:

1. The Comfort Zone isn't necessarily the enemy – but it is our default setting, and it does have a strong pull.
2. The Stretch Zone is where growth happens but climbing out of our Comfort Zone isn't enough to get there – we also need to make sure our Stretch ambition and Stretch commitments are aligned.
3. Once we enter the Stretch Zone, we don't automatically stay there. Focus and hard work is needed to stay 'stretchy'.
4. If your ambition is not matched by your commitment, you're a Dreamer with unrealistic expectations. If your commitment is not matched by your ambition and a coherent strategy to get there, you're a Latent, languishing in the area of missed opportunities. Neither of these zones are fulfilling or sustainable.
5. Staying in the Stretch Zone requires us to focus on all seven dimensions of Stretch. We are only ever as strong as our weakest link.

CHAPTER 1: **SCOPE**

- Exploring the mysteries of motivation
- Finding your Stretch Zone sweet spot: which kind of Stretch is right for you?
- The power of planning

We all have aspirations in life. It's one of the simple things that makes us human. But how do we know that these are the right aspirations *for us*? When we set ourselves a Stretch challenge, do we really understand what achieving that goal means on a day-to-day basis, or are we too consumed with thoughts of the finishing line? Grand ambitions take time to play out – but are we prepared to think through how those days might be spent, or do we only have our eyes on the end goal? When our amateur runner wakes up one morning and decides that they're going to take the bull by the horns, lift themselves out of their Comfort Zone and stretch, how does he know that the marathon is the event for him? Why not a half marathon? Why not a hundred metre relay? Why, in fact, running at all? Laying out the boundaries of your own SCOPE is about finding the right aspiration for you, but – much more than that – it's about knowing what that *means*. In this chapter, we'll delve into the different types of Stretch available to you, unpick the science of motivation that makes us all tick – and, most importantly, explore the way we can all prioritise the manifold possibilities out there, and zone in on the aspiration that's right for us. It is the start of the Stretch Journey and one which often gets skipped in the excitement of getting started. Get ready to scope out the Stretch Zone Sweet Spot...

Anything In Life Worth Having

It was Andrew Carnegie, the Scottish-American industrialist who led the expansion of the American steel industry in the late 19th century, who said, 'Anything in life worth having is worth working for.' At its peak, Carnegie's wealth was reckoned to reach to over $300 billion in today's money, an amount which would make him the richest person in the world now by some $240 billion. But Carnegie's wealth was hard won. This was a man who understood that building businesses takes time. Carnegie made that vast fortune when he sold his Carnegie Steel Company to JP Morgan at the age of 65, having started working in his teenage years – and, though the modern globalised marketplace can accelerate a company's growth spectacularly, the same principle applies today. Great successes often happen somewhere along a journey, but not often as that journey's first step.

A more contemporary lesson comes from Angry Birds, the smartphone game which has been downloaded more than a billion times. From the outside, you would have been forgiven for thinking that its makers, the company Rovio, had struck gold early – but Angry Birds was, in fact, the 52nd game they produced. Theirs was another long road to success.

For yet another, look no further than Starbucks, now one of the world's biggest brands, with almost 24,000 outlets across the globe. Starbucks was founded in 1971 and, for the first sixteen years of its life, was restricted to a small chain of coffee houses in its home town of Seattle. This company, which now seems so part of our everyday lives, spent sixteen years working hard to create a strong position in one city, and a further twenty-nine spreading out across the world. That represents an extraordinary commitment.

The key point is that very few businesses can be described as overnight successes. Tech 'unicorns' like Air BnB and Uber – who each received $2bn investment in their last rounds of funding – are true sensations, but they are few and far between in terms of both their speed to scale and their sheer level of investment. What the likes of Starbucks and Rovio have in common is something as important now as it was in Carnegie's day: the people behind these companies, their driving forces, had a clearly-defined idea and, by aligning their commitments with their ambition, could forge realistic plans by which to reach the very top. These people knew their SCOPE: they knew *what* they were going to do and they knew *why*.

In the world of Stretchonomics, the same principles apply whether you want to build the next Facebook, found a new landscape gardening firm, achieve your black belt in karate or learn the art of hot air ballooning. If we start at the beginning, it is important to explore the mysteries of what motivates us to do the things we do and how this impacts the end result.

The Mystery of Motivation

Setting out in pursuit of a Stretch goal isn't easy. That's why we call it a Stretch. But understanding *what* you want to achieve – whether that's to enter a new market, run a marathon, lift the FA Cup or launch a business – is only part of the equation. More problematic still is knowing *why* we want it – because when things get tricky, as they surely will, motivation is the difference between quitting and redoubling our efforts. By digging a little deeper and knowing what motivates us to do the things we do, we're better positioned to know what kind of stretch is right for us and how we can maximise our chances of getting there.

Knowing what stretch is right for you, right now, isn't straight-forward. As human beings we're messy, complicated creatures, and understanding ourselves isn't necessarily high on our agenda – a fact which extends into the world of big business as well. Big businesses often throw themselves into a stretching plan or strategy purely because that's what's expected. Yet adhering to these business norms does not necessarily chime with the motivations of the business itself. A few years ago, we were hired by a firm (let's call them Company X) whose leaders had declared they were going to double its size every five years. The board member we met told us about the company's proud history: over 150 years it had grown to a significant scale, with a turnover of just under $1bn. Company X had always tried to be disruptive and innovative and had been responsible for an impressive number of high profile and successful new launches in their industry. However, in a relatively slow growing industry (with growth of mid to low single digits) their current challenge looked very, very ambitious.

At first, we looked for ways that the company could grow at a rate rapid enough to achieve their enormous targets. It soon became clear that the only way of doing this was based on large scale acquisitions of other businesses and massive investment. It's not easy to buy a big competitor or enter a market where you have no existing business, let alone then go on to create new categories in that market. If they followed this path, Company X would need to hire over 5,000 new employees, increase its investment in advertising, product development, and build new factories. The company would become unrecognisable.

The reality was that the plan was a poor fit with Company X's traditional roots, its thoughtful and considered way of making decisions. Perhaps the company hadn't chosen the right Stretch goal at all. Or, in Stretchonomics terms, they'd settled on *what* they wanted to do without properly interrogating *why*. This meant that they hadn't considered the true impact on the SCOPE of their business or their TARGETS (more of this to come in the next chapter). By digging a little deeper we were able to help them redefine what SCOPE meant to them. We were able to help them understand the right level and type of Stretch, identifying a way that they could challenge and push themselves without losing the core traditions and principles which made them special and had made them successful in the previous decades.

Understanding their motivation was the key to helping them

get back in the Stretch Zone, ready for the sustainable growth ahead. Ultimately it became clear that their motivations were not purely financial. They were interested in rewards which went beyond the cash and the growth. For them it was not about world domination. This was a classic example of a Stretch challenge, a balancing act between the things we want and the things we are prepared to do to get there.

Let's pick apart this idea of *motivation* a little further. Motivations, of course, can be somewhat different, depending on whether you're looking to stretch as an individual or as a corporation. Think back to our marathon runner. We can think of an individual's motivations as belonging, broadly speaking, to one of six areas:

6. **Incentive.** Money, they say, makes the world go round, and, for many of us, our incentives are financial: the bonus we'll receive at work, or the commission we earn on each transaction. But incentives go beyond the financial too. Perhaps you've been rewarded by a promotion for consistent good work, or had your contribution recognised by an award?

7. **Fear.** On the other side of incentive, is the fear of punishment that comes with failure. Students who are penalised for not achieving the appropriate grades and employees penalised for not making targets are all being motivated by fear. Think of **Incentive** and **Fear** as the 'carrot and stick' of motivation. But **Fear** doesn't have to be a bad thing. Chelsea manager Jose Mourinho may not have liked it when his Manchester United counterpart Alex Ferguson claimed that, like him, he had a fear of failure, but it's true – and it's one of the reasons for his un-paralleled success. By actively exploiting his fear of failure, Mourinho is able to keep driving his players on to further successes, and to combat the complacency that can often kick in after a championship win. For Mourinho, Ferguson,

McEnroe and others like them, fear of failure ensures they never lose their intensity of focus.

8. **Achievement.** The good feelings that come with accomplishment are natural to us all. Think of our marathon runner – the rich sense of satisfaction gained by proving our competency to ourselves is often what motivates us to get out of bed in the morning.

9. **Growth.** People who accumulate new experiences or learn new skills will often say that they're compelled to keep going by something deep inside. What they mean is that this is a truly intrinsic motivation. Remember this term – we'll be digging more deeply into it in our upcoming HUNGER chapter. The motivation to grow as individuals is often hard-wired into us, and that simple yearning for change can be enough to spur us onward. Setting new challenges is what motivates serial entrepreneurs like Elon Musk, whose businesses – PayPal, Tesla, SpaceX – all operate in different sectors.

10. **Power.** Being motivated by power might mean we want total authority over our own lives – or, more shadily, that we thirst to control the people around us. Being motivated by power alone often induces people to destructive behaviour and insular, short-term thinking. And we need look no further than Donald Trump's rise to the American presidency in 2016 for the perfect example of how the lust for power, pure and simple, can motivate someone to the highest office. Desiring power can be a proxy for the desire to control others – but it doesn't have to be a negative thing. It's worth remembering that the way we approach power can render it a force for good (even in an era of Brexit and Trump…).

11. **Social.** At the other end of the spectrum from **Power**, the desire to fit in with others, or the desire to buoy others up and help them succeed, can be a powerful motivation. Many sportspeople would attest to this clearly. How often do you hear a

sportsperson saying that they were spurred on to a great achievement because they did not want to let their team-mates down? And this isn't the preserve of sportsmen alone. Feeling a connection with the people around us is part of what makes us human.

In some ways identifying the motivations of a business is more complex. Businesses involve more people and often feel as 'the business' has a life of its own. A business's leadership needs to know why the business exists – what is the point, its reason for being? While this can lead us into the sometimes bizarre and murky world of 'visions', 'missions', 'BHAGs' (big hairy audacious goals), or even the current vogue of 'purpose', understanding why the business is looking to evolve and grow as the world around it changes is critical for long term success. Typically the motivations which drive business can be grouped in seven types:

1. **Maximising Profits.** We'll all be familiar with this one. Maximising profits has been the most popular motivation of business since time immemorial – but it's not the only one…

2. **Maximising Sales.** This differs from maximising profits in one key way: when a company is motivated by maximising sales, they're talking volume, not value. In its infancy, Netflix made huge losses generating content and buying shows for its platform to drive subscription rates; it didn't care about making profit, it only cared about ensnaring subscriptions. Or think of a company like Tesla, the electric-car manufacturer headed by serial entrepreneur Elon Musk. Tesla's stated aim of having 500,000 cars on the road by 2018 is an ambitious stretch target, and the motivation is sales, not profit – all as part of a deliberate programme to disrupt, build brand awareness, and position Tesla as a huge fixture in the automotive industry going into the future. This is often seen in new or emerging markets, where

short term sales growth is put ahead of longer term "monetisation" plans.

3. **Market Share.** New entrants into a stable or mature market will often value developing market share above profit and sales. Consider the example of supermarkets Aldi and Lidl entering the UK retail sector. Faced with a market dominated by the likes of Tesco, Sainsbury's, Asda – and, at the higher end, Waitrose and M&S – Aldi and Lidl committed themselves to aggressive marketing, positioning themselves as quality supermarkets for the more budget-conscious consumer. For them, carving out a niche and a loyal consumer base was the primary motivation. By 2015, the firms already controlled 10% of the UK market for the first time – astonishing in the context of the four big players stealing single share points from each other for the preceding decades.

4. **Survival.** Dark times come. Recessions hit, driving consumer spending down. New challengers arrive in a market, intensifying the competition. And, as happened in the oil industry when crude oil prices permanently plunged, firms – including some of our own clients – have to resort to a survival footing. Since 2014, the major players in the oil industry have focused on cutting costs to such an extent that non-critical spending has halved. This has not been a huge amount of fun for those companies involved but it has been essential. Survival can be a powerful motivator in the corporate world. However, some have warned that, by slashing their budgets for exploration, larger energy companies might never have the strength to return to the profitability they once had.

5. **Shareholder Value.** The structure of many businesses demands that they think primarily in terms of their shareholders' financial returns. Yet, when we're motivated by satisfying our shareholders – which, for many larger listed companies, means hitting quarterly earnings targets – there is an obvious danger

that thinking in such a short time frame stops everyone seeing the bigger picture. In smaller companies this might be a question of personal finance or expectation of the founding team, or it might fit with investors' expectations of payback – how much 'value' they are they expecting and when. This motivation is often a balancing act between short term gratification, and a longer term vision.

6. **The Social Good.** Being motivated by the social good might not directly tie in to the profitability of a business, but it can still be a strong motivating factor. We worked with two homeopaths who had launched their own skin-care brand and were seeking to grow it. The primary motivation of their company was ethical – to benefit the consumer with natural remedies, and be less harmful to the environment – but our challenge was to look beyond this and translate it into a coherent business strategy for sustainable growth. Being ethically motivated does not preclude the possibility of profit, but typically, a balance must be struck. We increasingly see consumer brand businesses claiming to exist for higher purposes. Unilever, a leading proponent of this approach sees its 'purpose' driven brands – those with a wider view of how and why they exist beyond pure financials – growing at twice the rate of 'regular' brands.

7. **Satisficing.** To satisfice is to incorporate several different objectives at once, without attempting to maximise any particular one, so inherently there is compromise. Businesses motivated by 'satisficing' might, at one and the same time, want to profit their shareholders *and* themselves. Yet, if they are particularly risk-averse, they often settle for a financial return that is 'just good enough' – not dramatically high, not dramatically low, but the right level to keep things 'ticking over'. Retail banks, for instance, rarely invest in the kind of infrastructure they need to elevate the relationships they have with their consumers; for them, the financial return isn't worth the effort – so, instead,

they prefer to close branches and, in doing so, retreat to their Comfort Zones. This is a dangerous course to pursue long term and those who do are often vulnerable to changes in the competitive and market contexts.

It isn't easy to understand our motivations, but it *is* important – and much of our work has focused on helping companies interrogate the assumptions they have about who they are and why they do the things they do. Big business provides a great wealth of experience, but it's equally fascinating to work with entrepreneurs and small-to-medium sized businesses, because for these people personal and business motivations often overlap. One entrepreneur we worked with was launching his own brand – but it was unclear initially whether his motivations were to grow the business quickly, maximising sales, to create a nice "lifestyle" business or to reconnect with his family's heritage in the industry. As a consequence the original business plan lacked clarity and sense of purpose – he knew what he wanted to do but it wasn't clear why! It was only by drilling down and defining what his motivation actually was that he could devise a crystal-clear strategy and properly embark on his Stretch. Our first step was to understand him better, before we then looked at his business, the idea or the market in which he was set to operate.

Confronting what our true motivations are can be a difficult and even painful challenge but, whenever we embark on a Stretch, interrogating the *why* is an important factor in determining the *what*. Some Stretch goals are challenging and require more commitment than others. If the motivation for this isn't right, you need to know this at the earliest possible juncture. Think back to our Company X, and it's plain to see how a company that isn't aware of its motivation might stride off in pursuit of a Stretch goal that isn't 'right' for them. This could have been very expensive at best – and, at worst, it could have damaged the business considerably.

The First Type of Stretch

In Stretchonomics there are three fundamental types of growth challenge. Each one is distinct, and each one has its own different advantages.

Our first type of Stretch is one with which you might feel familiar: the stretch to get better at what we already do. In business this might mean growing your market share, expanding into new territories or making the business more efficient – while, for individuals, it might mean enhancing an existing skill set, like our amateur runner who decides to take on the challenge of running a marathon. Getting better at what you already do might seem like an easy option, but anyone who's ever taken a long hard look at themselves and decided to *improve* will tell you how daunting it can actually be. Many of our own clients avoid this option, either because it doesn't seem 'sexy', exciting or daring enough – or because they believe they're doing everything they already can. But the fact of the matter is: very few of us are.

So – how do we go about improving the things we already do, perhaps things at which we're already proficient? First things first: it isn't easy.

In 2013, this was precisely the situation with which global fast food giant McDonalds was faced. McDonalds has always been an aggressively expansionist business, but across the last years they had seen the revenue from their drive-through restaurants in the USA drop spectacularly. At the time, drive-through sales accounted for 70% of all McDonalds revenue, so this drop-off was hitting their core business hard. And it soon became apparent why: McDonalds measures the average time it takes to get through their drive-throughs in seconds, and in 2013 their average speed was 189 seconds, or a little over 3 minutes. One of their major rivals, Wendy's, had an average a full 30 seconds faster. Seconds, McDonalds now had evidence to see, mattered. But how to fix this problem?

McDonald's CEO was a passionate believer in the power of incremental change – a strategy he'd adopted from the manufacturing field. Even the tiniest change to a manufacturing method, can, over time, make a vast change to a company's fortunes. Or, to put it more plainly: every little thing adds up. For McDonald's this meant interrogating the things they were doing at the drive through and asking what could be changed to permit further growth. What effect would a less complex menu, with fewer choices, have on the speed of decisions being made in a drive through queue, and the speed with which those orders could be delivered? Could something as small as simplifying the menu board speed up the decision making and reduce the time each customer was waiting? If each small fix like this contributed a single percentage point to overall speed and efficiency, what might the results look like over a whole day, a week, a financial year? When we stretch like this, we have to keep in mind – like McDonald's did – that a stretch does not happen overnight; stretching like this can be about having ourselves constantly attuned to ways to improve our existing methods. It's a commitment to a long term goal, enacted over a breadth of time – not a singular dramatic, headline grabbing, change.

This is true, not only in the world of business, but in the world of professional sport as well. When Dave Alred, the sports coach credited with helping Jonny Wilkinson become the best dead-ball kicker in rugby, began working with the golfer Luke Donald, he knew there were challenges to be faced. As an introverted character, Donald needed to be shown specific ways to progress his game, and Alred responded by conducting detailed analysis of Donald's methods, identifying ways they could add value to his game in a plethora of different areas. 'You have to be prepared to accept the ugly areas and put in the work in,' Alred famously said. After working with Alred and paying attention to the small fixes – getting a little bit stronger, fine-tuning the accuracy of his shots –

Donald climbed to the top of the world rankings in 2011; and, when he stopped working with Alred in 2012, claiming that over-analysis of his performance was ruining his game, he quickly slipped out of the world rankings altogether, with the 2012 BMW PGA being his last significant achievement. Doing the same but better can often involve breaking things down to build them back up – and that is not an easy thing for a multi-national corporation or for individuals.

The Second Type of Stretch

We've looked at the challenges of improving what we already do, but now let's stretch a little further. Our second type of Stretch challenge demands that we think a little more laterally, by taking the things we're already good at and applying them to a different, unfamiliar field. For a business this might mean expanding into adjacent markets, as Apple did when they moved from building computers, to portable music devices to smartphones – while, for individuals it might mean a career change, or setting up a business of your own.

This is a type of stretch with which we're very familiar. We first met as consultant and client in 2001 when, instructed by our respective bosses to work on a particularly ambiguous and thorny innovation challenge, we went for dinner to see if red wine and steak would help us unlock some answers. Conversation turned to our various frustrations. We were both pretty young and looking to get on; and we had a remarkably similar view of what was wrong and right in our industry – and also what we might like to do differently. Our respective jobs were rewarding (at least financially) and, in some ways, we were both in safe, sensible set-ups. Perhaps we could both have continued in that way for the rest of our careers – but that evening we decided to set up a business of our own. That was the evening that, over good wine and terrible food, we agreed the principles and approaches which would become out first business – *Mangrove*. We knew that setting up a consulting firm of our own wouldn't be easy, but we had a clear idea of what we wanted to achieve and, with the experience and contacts we could each bring to the table, we believed we had at least a chance of success. Yet, this move was not without its perils. We each had partners, families and friends who needed us; we each had lives beyond consulting that we wanted to maintain; we knew that we were not the sort of people who needed or wanted to work 24 hours a day, seven days a week. But nor were we the sort of people who were content to sit back and allow our careers to play out around us. We wanted the opportunity to do new things, to take new risks, to be beholden only to ourselves. Perhaps we did not articulate it at the time, but we had stepped into our own Stretch Zone by adopting this second type of stretch: using our existing skill-sets to go out and build something new.

The degree of commitment required to make this kind of growth strategy successful can be greater than with our first type of stretch, and it's likely to involve some more unknowns as well. Samsonite, famous for their high-quality and durable suitcases and other items of luggage, famously decided to diversify after the 1929 Wall Street Crash decimated their core business. By applying their expertise in lightweight steel frames and injection moulding, they were able to move beyond suitcases and make significant gains in the folding chair and furniture sector. This other side of the business even eclipsed their core suitcase sales briefly – and, although it has stopped producing furniture today, it still supplements its luggage with umbrellas, wallets and other paraphernalia.

It's crucial that, when we adopt this kind of stretch, we're in full command of who we are: what our strengths are, what our weaknesses are, and how they can be exploited in other arenas. We stretched ourselves in this way by founding Mangrove, but we have gone on to help other companies commit similar stretches as well –

and it has taken us all over the world, from Shanghai to Sao Paulo, Kenya to Kuwait, via Islamabad, Accra, New York, and Slough.

There are over 180 million people in Nigeria (the exact numbers are unknown). The population is roughly split evenly between Christians in the south – which includes the troubled oil-rich delta area – and Muslims in the north. The country's largest city, and the jewel in its crown, is Lagos, a thoroughly modern African city: noisy, busy, bustling and full of life and energy. From the moment you arrive at the airport until your plane home takes off, Lagos is an assault on the senses which is as exhilarating as it is exhausting.

In Nigeria, over half of the population don't drink alcoholic beverages, with alcohol being forbidden under Islamic law and frowned upon by fast growing evangelical Christian churches. Our client had a long history in Nigeria, predominantly as a brewer. Breweries only really make money when they're busy – they are expensive to run, so operating close to capacity is important to being profitable. Working with our client we explored the idea of selling drinks to the other 50% of the population for whom beer was not an option, and in the process, keep the breweries running as close to permanently as we could.

We helped the company use their brewing assets to enter the world of soft drinks. They already knew about creating amazing tasting drinks and highly desirable consumer brands. Our plan was that they should utilise these skills to create a range of non-alcoholic, brewed soft drinks, something a bit more special and grown-up than Coke and Pepsi, something that suggested style and sophistication. The first launch happened in Kenya, and the first four months resulted in 7m bottles being sold. The company had been able to redefine their SCOPE and repurpose their current assets and knowledge to create a new line of business.

This kind of stretch demands a higher level of commitment than our first, but there is a kind of stretch that goes even further...

The Third Type of Stretch

Few individuals have reinvented themselves as many times as Arnold Schwarzenegger. A bodybuilder at 15, the winner of the coveted Mr Universe title at 20, Arnie went on to reimagine himself not only as a Hollywood leading man but, in even more of a departure, the Republican governor of the state of California. From bodybuilder, to actor, to politician, Arnie has shown himself to be the perfect exemplar of our third type of stretch. Because… here's where things get the stretchiest of all. Let's do what Arnie did, and explore ways of doing something completely different.

For a business this might mean developing radical innovations or acquiring other businesses to take the company in new directions. An individual, meanwhile, might decide that running is no longer the sport for them and decide to throw themselves headlong into cycling, swimming or a triathlon instead. Stretches as ambitious as this can often mean pushing the boundaries of our commitments and can test motivations. Sometimes we have to be willing to go out there and find new ideas, or fresh thinking, to incorporate into our own endeavours – we'll be exploring many of the methods that can be adopted here in our later TECHNIQUE chapter – while other times we have to acknowledge that we don't have the assets, capabilities and people to properly tackle a growth opportunity like this, and we'll be exploring what our options are here when we look at the stretchiness of our RESOURCES. These kinds of stretch aren't for everyone, and it's important to know, too, that taking bigger risks and stretching more fully doesn't necessarily lead to a more profitable outcome. Stretchonomics is not about encouraging everyone to dial up their ambitions; it's about zoning in on the ambition that's right for you. Diversification and reinvention can be fulfilling adventures to embark upon, but the commitments they require are vast. Knowing what our motivations are will help us identify if this is the stretch for us.

Stretching in this way might also mean entering into partnerships with other companies who have expertise in an area we don't. In 1997, the British supermarket chain Tesco decided that there was an opportunity for them in the retail banking sector, and so Tesco Personal Finance was born. Yet Tesco knew their market and, crucially, knew their limitations as well. Realising they didn't have the skills or infrastructure to found a new bank alone, they forged a partnership with Royal Bank of Scotland (RBS) and, by utilising their expertise, were able to launch their own successful retail bank. Then, in 2008, when they felt they had incorporated all of the relevant RBS expertise into their own company, they bought out RBS and created their own version of the infrastructure RBS had once provided. Tesco Bank, as it is now called, has 7 million customers in the UK alone and has moved its operations out of stores and exclusively online – a truly modern retail bank.

Joint ventures like this don't just mitigate the risk of our third type of stretch; they show a willingness to move beyond our comfort zones, to embrace big, sweeping changes – it is often very hard for big companies to work together like this. We were hired by a large global automotive brand, and helped them stretch by creating a venture group to look at investing in start-ups to explore new and challenging ideas. The group invests in companies whose aim is to disrupt the automotive and mobility worlds, rewarding them with capital investment as well as the resources, expertise and networks of the industry giant. As a venture capital firm, they're working with smaller firms and start-ups while simultaneously managing an industry giant exploring new technologies and emerging markets.

Whether you're stretching by acquiring a new business, hiring some outside help, or entering into a joint venture with another firm, what characterises this kind of stretch most of all is the act of reinvention. What got you to the place you are now is unlikely to be the thing that will take you on the next stage of your growth journey. Hold this in your head for a moment – because this is fundamental to the spirit of Stretchonomics.

Reinvention can come in many forms, and one of its most potent is the willingness to simply abandon something that's no longer working. Remember Posh Spice? Victoria Beckham began her career as one of the Spice Girls, the pre-packaged pop group that crashed into the music scene in the mid-1990s. But when fame and a musical career didn't last – Victoria tried to launch a solo career after the Spice Girls disbanded, but the same kind of success did not follow – she threw herself instead into the world of fashion, looking to build something out of a very personal passion. Was she taken seriously when she set out? No. Is she now the owner of a multimillion dollar fashion empire? In a word: yes. Beckham had the confidence to turn her back on one career and launch herself into another. Love her or loathe her, it's an impressive turnaround which required huge commitment of time, money and talent.

Reinvention might also come with a little bit of what we call 'positive ruthlessness', the kind Steve Jobs had when he returned to Apple in 1997 after twelve years away. Jobs' first order of business was to strip away *all* of Apple's peripheral products and, instead of continuing to produce a broad range, concentrate on only four core items. It was a decision that elevated Apple's fortunes and made the future iPod, iPad, and iPhone the gadgets of choice in the current market: reinvention of a brand's focus itself.

This might be the most challenging stretch of them all, but when our ambitions and commitments are aligned there is no need to think this out of your grasp. Challenging as it may be, it is still a path well-trodden. Track cyclist Victoria Pendleton reimagined herself as a jockey, and went on to race in the 2016 Foxhunter Chase at Cheltenham – where she defied many expectations and finished in fifth place. Redefining what she wanted to achieve completely was no easy feat – it meant starting at the bottom, accepting that, although she had been on top of the world as a track cyclist, she was a novice in this new arena. And she's not alone: Rebecca Romero moved from cycling into the world of rowing, footballer Michael Owen is now also a jockey, Bradley Wiggins, the Olympic cyclist, is now retraining as a rower. Musicians like David Bowie and Madonna, as familiar as they are with acts of musical reinvention, have made the move from musician to actor and back again. Ronald Reagan, 40th President of the United States, began his career as a broadcaster and Hollywood actor, and ended it as leader of the free world. Donald Trump, the 45th, went from dubious businessman and walk-on film star (look out for him in Home Alone 2!), to TV reality star with *The Apprentice*, and finally to global twitter goofball. If that isn't a stretch, tell us what is!

The Possibilities Parade

How do we settle on which kind of stretch is the right one for us? How does our runner know he should be attempting a marathon instead of training to swim the English Channel? We live in a world where the choices we're faced with can sometimes feel endless. How do we stop ourselves being paralysed by choice?

Making the right decision demands we approach ourselves with a brutal kind of honesty, and it begins with two simple questions:

1. What do I want out of it?
and
2. What am I prepared to put into it?

Ask yourself the first question. It's going to help you highlight your options, out of all the many thousands out there. Then ask yourself the second – because this is the one that really focuses us on what's realistic *for us*. Keep those two questions in mind: they're at the very heart of Stretchonomics.

If you've ever read the F Scott Fitzgerald classic, *The Great Gatsby*, you might remember Nick Carraway, the world war one veteran and novice businessman who gets sucked into the world of the mysterious socialite after whom the novel is named. For Carraway, there are four types of people in life: 'the pursued, the pursuing, the busy, and the tired.' Those who've already achieved the things they set out to do are the pursued: they're at the head of the pack, being chased by younger pretenders, the 'pursuing'. Behind them are the 'busy' – which might just be another watchword for the lazy among us, the dreamers who might know what they want but aren't motivated to get there. Meanwhile, trailing even further behind – last but not least – are the tired, demoralised people who have given up on their dreams. We all know somebody like this: these are the people who simply take reality as it is and go through life without finding out how far they can really go.

Picture Carraway's types of people and where they might sit in our stretch chart. The pursued are up there at the top of the Stretch Zone, the pursuers not far behind, while the busy dreamers are outside the Stretch Zone, in that place where ambition is not matched by commitment – and the tired, demoralised among us are somewhere in the Comfort Zone, perhaps even atrophying away.

We can locate businesses and other organisations on our stretch chart in a similar way. Most of the businesses we work with want to be at the very top of the Stretch Zone, pioneering new products and markets, doing new and exciting things – underpinned by big ambitions for growth. Yet surprisingly few are prepared to do what's really needed to get there. When faced with taking risks, or investing ahead of the curve, they hold back. They are ambitious in spirit, but their behaviour is much more risk averse. They haven't hit the Stretch Zone sweet spot, that place where ambitions and commitments match.

Look around you and you'll see this in your everyday lives as well. If you've ever set yourself a challenge without really considering the implications, you're far from alone. Losing a couple of stone to look good on holiday is an attractive prospect, but how prepared are people for the sacrifices that this involves? The change in routine, the cravings, the need to say 'no' on multiple occasions – these are the things that often derail a dieter who's set out with exemplary intentions. Or consider the desk worker with a sedentary lifestyle who wants to get fit. If that person sets themselves the challenge of completing a marathon, are they really ready for the weeks and months of early starts, the aching muscles and stiff legs? As a species we are often guilty of setting ourselves a challenge to accomplish a great thing, when what we really mean is *we wish we had already done that.* Having the ambition to run a marathon is not only about holding an image of crossing the finishing line in your mind. What the ambition to run a marathon really looks like is: getting up out of bed before your loved ones, long lonely runs, sore backs and even sorer legs. If you're not really prepared to do all that, then perhaps marathon running isn't for you.

And do you know what? Perhaps that's alright. It may sound sacrilegious, but many of us might be better off setting our sights a little bit lower, dialling back the ambition – if only for now. This doesn't mean you'll never run a marathon. It doesn't mean you'll never achieve your black belt in karate – or cross the Pacific Ocean in a rowing boat like Laura Penhaul and her crew. Defining your SCOPE is not about chasing impossible dreams and ambitions. It's about setting the right goal – one which challenges us, but one that's still achievable, one that won't be so punishing we give up.

The truth is, we cannot all strive for our goals in the way internationally competitive athletes do, with their entire life taken up by their quest. We are not built to live that kind of life, to prioritise one specific goal over everything else, and we should neither try nor pretend that we are. Modern life is busy. It's frenetic. We have demanding work lives, families we don't want to neglect, friends we don't want to let drop out of our lives. These things are important – and we should never be tricked into thinking that, just because we don't prioritise our stated ambition over these things, we are not doing enough. A goal that's realistic *to us* is much more valuable than one that goes beyond our commitments and capabilities, because it's a goal in which we can realistically invest.

And it's the same in business. We've seen, time and again, how businesses set unrealistic growth targets without fully considering the ramifications of what that means. Unrealistic expectations lead to a lack of motivation, unhappiness, and an unwillingness to Stretch in the future. A business whose stretch ambition was never realistic will often fail to invest the necessary resources in their project, for the simple reason that they didn't know what was required in the first place. Then the business's directors will wonder why their targets were missed. This kind of failure is completely avoidable. Realistic goals might lead to steady rather than spectacular growth, but that is much better than failure. The top right of the Stretch Zone is not for everyone – and this is a lesson for us all, whether we're out on our first training run or Mark Zuckerberg looking to make Facebook's next move.

Planning Permission

If you knew a little about the author F Scott Fitzgerald, perhaps you know a little about Miguel de Cervantes too. Cervantes' defining novel, *Don Quixote*, follows the Spanish nobleman Alonso Quixano – who, upon deciding to bring chivalry back to the land, sets out under the *nom de plume* Don Quixote to right wrongs and perform knightly deeds. Don Quixote himself is famous for 'tilting at windmills', losing himself in flights of fancy, but his creator Cervantes also imbued him with a mantra that might even have been written with Stretchonomics in mind: 'the person who has a plan, has half their battle won.'

Knowing what you want to do and why you want to do it is the first stride in defining your SCOPE, but equally important is knowing what that looks like in practise. What are the tangible steps you need to take to achieve a stretch ambition? Do these match your capabilities and commitments along the way? How can we possibly know what it takes to get where we want to go... unless we plan it first?

Plans are vital to the success of any stretch ambition. And, in fact, the results of a significant study show that the mere act of writing a business plan *doubles* our chances of achieving our ambitions.[3] This particular study showed that formulating a plan beforehand – whether that plan was deviated from or not – increased the success of all manner of business goals, whether that was making a significant acquisition, attracting investment, or simply growing the company.

In our experience, a plan is like a map. When you're following a plan, you can see how much progress you've made and how far you are from your destination. Better armed, you can better make decisions on where to go or what to do next. Only when you have a plan can you properly ring-fence the space and time that's required to achieve your stretch goals. Without a plan, how can we focus our time and energies on the appropriate behaviours to fulfil our ambition? Without a plan, we're prone to letting the day to day distractions of life draw us away from the commitments we need to make in order to succeed.. We can't put it better than Yogi Berra, the famous baseball player turned coach, when he said, 'If you don't know where you're going, you'll end up somewhere else.'

The Secrets of Scope

SCOPE is only one of the seven different dimensions of Stretch, but before we go on to investigate TARGET, let's look back at the secrets of Scope:

1. Before you set out on your journey, you need to decide on your stretch challenge.

2. The first step on this voyage is to understand what's driving your to stretch. Whether you're acting as a business or as an individual, what are your motivations?

3. There are three fundamental types of ways to stretch. Each demands varying degrees of commitment: doing more of the same thing; redeploying your assets to a new arena; or stretching the furthest and doing something genuinely new.

4. Consider each option and then decide what kind of stretch is right for you. To do so, ask yourself the two most important questions: what do I want out of it, and what am I prepared to put in?

5. Never underestimate the value of planning – it can double your chances of success.

CHAPTER 2: **TARGET**

- Fulfilment as the definition of success
- The cougar in the car: the difference between 'growth' and 'fixed' mind-sets
- Applying the 40% rule by setting the bar higher

Defining our ambitions isn't just about deciding on *what* we want to do – we have to be able to define *how* ambitious we're going to be in our chosen field. Think back to our runner. He's chosen his event by defining his SCOPE, and he's going to run a marathon. Now he needs to ask himself another big question: how quickly am I going to run it? What is the right TARGET?. Should he be aggressive and set himself a semi-professional three-hour time? Or should he go easy on himself and just look to finish? How can our marathon runner nail down what the right time is for him?

We are all confronted by this same decision. If your SCOPE is the direction in which you're headed, your TARGET defines how far along that road you're going to travel and at what speed. How ambitious do you want to be? On the surface this may seem a simple question, but if there's one thing that we've learned through a decade and a half of Stretchonomics, it's that setting useful targets is more difficult than it seems.

Others have derived ways of setting helpful targets, and perhaps the best known is the idea of SMART goals, 'popular' in the exciting, non-stop world of project management. A SMART goal is one that is **S**pecific, **M**easurable, **A**greed, **R**ealistic and **T**ime-bound – or, in other words, has a clear ambition and clear boundaries in which to achieve it. So far, so helpful – but an ambition might align with all the SMART criteria and still not be the right one for you and your business. In Stretchonomics, we have identified four distinct criteria and, by interrogating each, we can tell if a goal is right for you. In Stretch, we think of your TARGET as being the thing that propels you along. We think of it as being your FUEL:

- **F**ulfilling: we must think of fulfilment as a definition of success, and not solely be driven by statistics/
- **U**ncomfortable: if it feels uncomfortable, good! It means you're reaching for something new and it's liable to push you into your Stretch Zone.
- **E**xpressive: whatever your TARGET is, let it create a sense of identity. Make it motivating!
- **L**earning-focused: a good TARGET should be built around a growth mind-set and not being afraid to 'fail'.

What does all this mean? How can we harness this FUEL and let it direct us toward the best and most appropriate TARGET for us? How can we derive a definition of success that is fulfilling? And what is the conscious change in mind-set that will help you unlock the potential for unlimited growth? This chapter will explore each of these aspects in turn, and propel you along the way to defining the right TARGET for you.

Fulfilment is the Definition of Success

Denis Waitley, the author and motivational speaker, has a quote which has always stayed lodged in our minds: 'It is not in the pursuit of happiness that we find fulfilment,' he said, 'but in the happiness of pursuit.'

This maxim has never been more relevant for our times. Once upon a time, it was easier to define a simple notion of 'success.' There was an age, not so very long ago, when success was dictated by the numbers on a balance sheet, the accounts at the end of a financial year – or where success was a simple binary thing: did I get the promotion or not? Such is the baby boomer, Gen X mind-set – but with the much analysed 'millennial' mind-set now impacting how we all think, most of us would acknowledge that life is more complex. Consequently, the definition of success has changed, becoming much more multifaceted, incorporating emotional wellbeing, mental health, and the opportunity to do what you love rather than solely what is expected of you. Nowadays, then, there is no single definition of success in business, work or personal life. For some people it might still be about attaining wealth, fame or respect – but it is now more generally accepted that there is no one universal way to define 'success'.

Perhaps this is why happiness and self-fulfilment are becoming more important in people's lives. There is no job for life, there is a declining trust in the big institutions that used to employ the majority of the population – and, what's more, the corporate career is under pressure. In fact, 60% of UK employees work for small or medium-sized companies – and this, just like self-employment, is a figure which continues to grow. Concern for wellbeing, acceptance of individuality and a world of opportunities have led us to a point where we have a more rounded, balanced and positive way of defining targets in life. It's often written about as a millennial mind-set, and yet it appeals to many more people than those born in the 1990s: if we can no longer define success in a material way, how then do we define it?

Setting a TARGET in Stretchonomics does not mean bench-marking yourself against others. As human beings it seems we are hard-wired to that 'grass is always greener' feeling – the niggling idea that things might be better on the other side of the fence, or that somebody else has it better than we do. Instagram, Facebook and Twitter have a wonderful way of compounding this. But comparing ourselves to others' success always has a negative impact on us. The Stretchonomics answer is to benchmark yourself, not against the achievements of others, but against your expectations of yourself. Your opponent is not the person whose business is eclipsing yours or the runner who runs faster. Your opponent is the things you want of yourself, the things tantalisingly out of grasp at the top of your Stretch Zone. Competing against an image of yourself propels us to achieve on our own terms, while competing against others is a vicious circle, prompting us to question our own worth.

Success comes in many forms, all particular to the person looking to define it, but there's one thing that unifies all those various and wide-ranging definitions of success. And that's a sense of personal fulfilment. What use is an extra million pounds to a city financier if he still looks at the other, wealthier people around him and feels a lack of joy or contentment? What use is running a marathon ten minutes faster than your personal best if all you wanted to do was finish ahead of your friends or club mates?

The key to getting the best out of Stretchonomics is to understand that happiness is a big part of success, and that expectations are key to happiness – wellbeing is driven not by how well things are going but by how things are going *relative* to our expectations. Take this to heart when you try and define what your TARGET might be. The right TARGET is not necessarily the one that comes with the greatest wealth, the fastest time, the world-breaking record attached. If it isn't fulfilling, is it really the right TARGET for you?

It's All In The Mind

After a long and illustrious career, there comes a point in an athlete's life when they must hang up their boots, spikes or any other bits of kit and retire from the professional circuit. Unlike most of us, athletes tend to retire in their 30s, when many of them still have their whole lives ahead of them. Professional sport is an all-encompassing thing. To excel, athletes have almost always been consumed with their chosen discipline since childhood. They have lived it, breathed it, eaten it and slept it for all of their lives. It has come to define them – and then, at a very early juncture, it's gone.

It's no coincidence that athletes often struggle at the point of retirement. Unhappiness, even depression, is common among retired sportspeople. Some say that these athletes miss the excitement of competition, the glory of winning, the bright lights of fame. Some say that they miss the camaraderie of their team mates, the reflected glory of winning, or the physical highs that training can bring. But we would argue that there is a common element behind all post career challenges: the sense of non-fulfilment that is often due to no longer having a relevant TARGET in their lives. Retired athletes have to adapt and identify new goals to go on and forge successful second careers. For those who manage to do so, their new idea of success may look considerably different to how it used to when they were scoring goals, breaking records or winning championships – but it will have one significant underlying factor in common: it will be *personally fulfilling*. We're not all retired athletes, but we have spent some time with former athletes with different backgrounds, from Olympians to World Cup winners across a range of sports, and the patterns are striking and relevant to those of us not in elite sport.

According to one major study, not having a relevant – and, importantly, a *specific* – goal in life is a major factor in developing depression and other mental health issues.[4.] People with goals that are too vague are by nature less motivated to achieve them – and people who are less motivated to achieve their goals are less likely to experience good feelings of success, which only serves to compound the negative images they hold of themselves. A specific goal has an explicitly stated end-point, while a general goal is too abstract to talk about, except in very general terms. A marathon runner who looks to complete the race in under 4 hours has a specific target, while somebody whose goal is 'to get fit' is being abstract – because they haven't asked themselves what 'get fit' means to them; it doesn't have a tangible beginning, middle and end. Not having a specific target is, in the worst cases, almost like not setting a target at all. The runner who aims to complete a 4 hour marathon has a good barometer by which to measure his success, and can break down his training regime accordingly, but the runner who just aims to 'get fit' doesn't have any measure by which to gauge his or her progress or success; the result is a lack of motivation, inertia and dissatisfaction. After all, without a specific target, we can never access the gratification that comes with achieving something we've set out to do. As the cricket umpire Bill Copeland said, 'The trouble with not having a goal is that you can spend your life running up and down the field and never score!"

Having a *specific* goal, then, is crucial – but, of all the specific targets we might set, how do we know which one's right for us? Anyone who has had a goal imposed upon them by outside forces – whether that's at work or in the home – will know the challenges this can create. When we're not passionate about reaching a target, are we really engaged enough to achieve it?

According to another study, it's the difference between an 'alarm goal' and an 'optimal goal' that determines whether a target is right for us – and hence whether we have the right level of passion to achieve it.[5.] Alarm goals are the goals we have when we feel like we *have* to do something, when it's our alarm, or our anxieties, pushing us to achieve. They are fear driven. 'Optimal goals', meanwhile, are goals that we determine ourselves. These targets come from deep inside us. They are the extensions of our core values, our hopes, and the beliefs we hold about ourselves – what Abraham Lincoln called 'the better angels of our nature.' It doesn't mean they come without stresses, and it doesn't mean they won't challenge us – but it does mean that they are the things we *want* to achieve, the things we can look back on with a sense of pride and satisfaction in a job well done. Achieving an optimal goal is fulfilling because it adds to the picture we each hold of *who we are* and *what we want to be part of.*

In fact, setting the right goals can have profound effects for us – not just psychologically, but physiologically too. Whether our stretch goal is personal or business-oriented, the scientists agree: the process of establishing targets for ourselves changes the chemistry of the brain itself. We can actually *see* in the way the brain operates the benefits of having clear and realistic targets – and we can harness this knowledge to drive us toward the appropriate targets for us.

Four things happen to the human brain when goals are set and while we're striving to achieve them – and we think this is pretty amazing![6.]

1. The human brain cannot tell the difference between what we have and what we want. When we set ourselves a goal, a corner of the brain behaves as if we've *already* accomplished it – it conflates a 'want' with something we already 'have'. In simple terms: the mere act of setting a goal can produce the same kind of confidence and happiness we would normally associate with achievement. This is amazing and powerful, and crucial because...

2. The brain rewards us. Dopamine is the hormone that the brain releases every time we do something good. Biologically, it compels us to repeat good behaviour and, thus, ensure our long term survival. In neurological terms, this means that our brain rewards us for both achievements *and* for setting a goal, but...

3. The brain can punish us as well. If we don't achieve our goals, no dopamine is released, and this leads to a dispirited feeling taking hold. Worse still, the brain treats us as if we've failed to achieve a goal *up until the point* when we do actually realise it. The tension between success and failure dominates the brain. It's what can propel us to reach our targets. And yet...

4. It's also the thing that can hold us back. Sometimes, the brain can respond to the tension between its self-image (we've already succeeded!) and the reality (we've yet to succeed!) by flooding our bodies with stress and anxiety hormones. This can make us shut down or abandon our ambitions. And the brain has other ways of leading us astray as well. Too often, the brain can be *tricked* into rewarding us. If we're praised and complimented by other people, even without any reason for that praise, the brain reacts exactly as if we'd achieved something good, by releasing dopamine into our system. In the long term, this can reduce our hunger to achieve – because our brain is telling us *we've already achieved*.

Being aware of the way the brain both rewards and undermines us is crucial when we're honing in on what the right TARGETS are for us. Because of the tension that setting goals can create, it's naturally more comfortable for us to revert to the inertia of a 'let's just do our best' approach. This might insulate us from experiencing the pain of failing to reach a target, but it also denies us the experience of satisfaction – and the opportunity for growth – that comes with making progress toward a goal. Rather, we should look to the brain for help in honing in on the right TARGETs for us: targets that are the natural extension of our core beliefs and values; targets that can be broken down into a succession of smaller steps, to better manage the way the brain rewards us along the way; targets that can fulfil us in a fundamental way. Fulfilment, as we've already seen, is the very definition of success. A relevant target isn't easy to define – but it's priceless to the art of Stretch.

Target Doesn't Mean Destination

A somewhat contentious addition to the modern business lexicon is that of a 'Stretch Goal' – not to be confused with the principles outlined in this book, which are much less problematic! A Stretch

Goal is, at its worst, an ambition so wildly beyond expectation, so wildly beyond current capabilities, that it isn't realistic. Many (typically large) companies often set themselves a Stretch Goal as a kind of declaration: we can do amazing things; achieve the impossible; we will not settle for mediocrity; we will double our business; we will succeed where others (including our predecessors) have not. For fans of old British sitcoms, there is more than a touch of Del Boy's *bon mot* – 'this time next year Rodney, we'll be millionaires!' When we set a Stretch Goal too far, though, it becomes meaningless or even demotivating, especially when paired with no real change in resource, risk taking or approaches – more of this later.

We have seen, time and again, how setting a goal that is clearly beyond us can actually have a negative effect. When leadership teams set an over-stretching goal their belief is that a big ambition automatically creates big passion and drive. But often the opposite is true. A team set a goal that they think is clearly unrealistic will often not truly commit to achieving that goal. After all, why should they, if it's so unrealistic that, no matter what efforts they go to, they're unlikely to succeed? Why not revert to the comfort of a 'carry on regardless' approach – or even call bullshit on the whole idea and ignore it? We have seen both of these responses being 'applied' within the various divisions of our multinational clients. In this case, a Stretch Goal has had the opposite effect than was intended: it has worked, not to drive us up out of our Comfort Zones, but to actively *keep us there*. The enormity of a Stretch Goal can lead to a kind of paralysis, and kill any potential for growth.

There are three possible unwanted outcomes when we set a unrealistic goal. Two of these are laid out above (ignore it or call it out as a nonsense), but the third can open the door to the darker side of human nature. Individuals may choose to cheat, cut corners, explore unethical behaviours or take the wrong kinds of risks. Sometimes, when people are set unreasonable goals, these temptations begin to grow more and more powerful. For an obvious example, look no further then the Enron scandal of 2001 and the later global financial collapse of 2008. The Enron Corporation, an energy firm based in Texas in the United States, famously rewarded its executives with enormous bonuses if they achieved specific targets – which first precipitated risky behaviours, and then criminality. Consider too, doping in all manner of sports from cycling, athletics to the NFL, and think about bankers jailed for insider trading or the sales executives mis-selling products – all of these transgressions can be a result of targets quite clearly beyond individuals, teams or businesses.

But what if there's another way of thinking about this? What if there are some moments when a goal that's beyond us might be the very thing that we need? Used incorrectly, Stretch Goals debilitate and demotivate us, but they can also force us to think differently, to try new approaches and behaviours in order to achieve greater levels of performance. Tech giants like Google have entire divisions dedicated to the pursuit of Stretch Goals – with 'Google X' being a semi-secret unit devoted to 'moonshots', those radical departures or ideas that could disrupt an entire industry or change the world. Serial entrepreneur and business giant Elon Musk's aim to start sending manned missions to Mars privately might seem fanciful, but it's also forced his company SpaceX to develop new reusable rocket technologies thought impossible only years earlier. Closer to Earth, think of the American Southwest Airline, which set itself the Stretch Goal of reducing the waiting time at airport gates from a whole hour to only ten minutes. This goal went against all the accepted knowledge of the airline industry, but by completely reimagining its processes, and even the behaviour of its customers, Southwest succeeded and set a new standard by which the entire industry would be measured.

There are clearly times, then, when a Stretch Goal used properly can trigger positive rather than negative behaviour. It might inspire, rather than demotivate; it might force us out of our Comfort Zones and challenge us to incorporate new techniques, or to commit more acts of courage along the way. But there is a greater truth here, and it's one at the heart of target-setting in Stretchonomic. Once in a while, our target might not actually be a tangible destination. What if our target is to learn something about ourselves in the process, or to grow in a challenging but unusual way? Might setting an unrealistic bar *and* not making it actually be helpful, so long as it's well-intended and drives the appropriate behaviours? Is it, to put it bluntly, useful to fail?

There are several reasons why it might not be the end of the world if you don't achieve the TARGET you set out with. Achieving every goal means the goals you are setting for yourself are probably too easy; a missed goal can motivate us to strive harder the next time; and, because we live in the real world, with real world pressures, sometimes our priorities change. Life and business pressures might mean that, though you set out with one TARGET in mind, sticking to it inflexibly might no longer be the right thing to do. The world around us is in a constant state of change – being too inflexible in our outlook might do more bad than good. But, above all else, failing builds resiliency and can actually contribute to longer term successes.

When Sir Mo Farah ran his first marathon, he set one goal: he wanted to win. Second place didn't matter. He could have set himself all kinds of different targets, from breaking the British record to finishing in a certain time or in the top three, to name a few. But he didn't. Winning was what he wanted. Nothing else would do.

In the end, Sir Mo finished in eighth place, four minutes behind the eventual winner, with a time which was the fourth fastest ever by a Briton. By most people's standards, that is an incredible result. It was his first marathon, after all. But by Sir Mo's standards, this was a failure. Two years before he attempted the marathon, Sir Mo had won gold in both the men's 5,000 metre race and the men's 10,000 metre race at the 2012 London Olympics. With this behind him, winning a marathon – at 26 miles long, more than four times the distance of his greatest achievement – could be seen as a stretch, but one that he might be expected to have a good chance of accomplishing. And yet fail was exactly what he'd done.

As it happened, Sir Mo might have failed in his stated objective, but does that necessarily mean he failed outright? The fact is that, though winning the marathon might have been Sir Mo's principal aim, it wasn't a target in isolation. Two years previously, Sir Mo had accomplished one of his life's goals and won two gold medals at the 2012 Olympics. Running a marathon two years later was about pushing himself beyond his previous limits, of taking his performance as a runner to a new level. It wasn't just winning the marathon that mattered to Sir Mo. It was the way he went about trying and the very fact that he *did* try. The event and the way he approached it was part of ensuring he would still have the correct mind-set when the next Olympics came round in 2016.

In Sir Mo's case, the pursuit of a new goal meant he wasn't able to sit back and rest on past achievements. The pursuit of something new improved him. His mind-set – of relentlessly looking for the next challenge, no matter how daunting – would ensure that he remained ahead of everyone else in 2016. And do you know what? It did exactly that. Sir Mo went on to win gold medals in both the men's 5000 and 10,000 metre races for the second time in 2016. He had become only the second man in history to win the 'double double', an astonishing success. And his secret weapon in achieving this? Setting himself a target that may well have been beyond him, but which inspired him to grow, to develop, to learn things about himself along the way; and to be content with the idea that, sometimes, just sometimes, you don't have to succeed.

Sir Mo's story is here because we believe that complacency is a killer. When we become complacent, we stop stretching. What was once a stretch might start to become a routine – and, unless we redefine the target and look to grow and go again, we find ourselves unwittingly stationary. When we accomplish a goal, especially one to which we've dedicated a big portion of our life, there can sometimes be a tendency to think of it as 'final'. Well, as we've seen, missing a target you've been dedicated to can be a destabilising thing – even after you've been successful. And this is something to which another Olympic athlete, the American swimmer Michael Phelps, can easily attest. Phelps was on top of the world in 2008 when he swam his way to a record eight gold medals at the Beijing Olympics. His entire life had been building to this moment but, in its aftermath, things unravelled spectacularly across all corners of his life. Having achieved the target he had set for himself, his mind and motivation wandered. In 2012 he formally retired from swimming, declaring he no longer wanted anything to do with the sport. Close friends found him unrecognisable. He was arrested for driving under the influence of alcohol, photographed by tabloid paparazzi with drug paraphernalia, and worked his way through a series of fractious and failed relationships – earning himself a six month suspension from the US swimming team along the way. Phelps' epiphany came in 2014 when, in the wake of his second DUI arrest, he was undergoing a period of rehab. Resolving to give up alcohol and recommit himself to his swimming life was not easy, but by recalibrating and defining a new target – success at the 2016 Olympics in Rio de Janeiro – he was able to resolve many of his personal issues, finding the passion and focus he had been lacking, and by which he could order his life. The result? The Michael Phelps of 2017 is a different man to the tormented soul of five, six, seven years earlier. A further five gold medals, and a silver, was added to his record in Rio, and today he runs the Michael Phelps Foundation, promoting swimming to young people across the Americas, as well as sitting on the board of Medibio, a company devoted to diagnosing mental health disorders. And all because Michael Phelps had come to understand a simple truth: that our targets are not fixed and inflexible; they are dynamic; to keep on growing and keep on being fulfilled, we have to constantly monitor and assess them. What was good for us once is not necessarily what is good for us *now*. Our TARGETs can and must grow and change.

You Never Lose: You Win, Or You Learn

Responding to setbacks is a vital part of any Stretch journey. None of us can set out toward our targets and expect to get there without experiencing any hurdles along the way – and it's crucial that we're not only prepared for the failures that might come our way, but that we don't let them influence how we establish our TARGET. The basketball superstar Michael Jordan famously 'owned' his own failures when he said, 'I've missed more than 9000 shots in my career. I've lost almost 300 games. 26 times, I've been trusted to take the game winning shot and missed. I've failed over and over and over again in my life. And this is why I succeed.' And he's not the only one.

How Sir Mo conquered the historic 'double double' is in part down to the rigours he was able to put his body through – but even more important than that is the way he approached the process mentally. And, while we might not all have the physical prowess of Sir Mo Farah, we do all have access to the mind-set that spurred him on his way.

Dr Carole S. Dweck, world-renowned Stanford University psychologist, is a master of mind-sets. Dweck – who began her academic career at Barnard in 1967 and achieved her PhD at Yale in 1972 – has studied the sciences of motivation and character all of her life and her defining work concerns the difference between what she calls a 'fixed' and 'growth' mind-set. According to Dweck, those of us with a fixed mind-set assume that our character, intelligence and creative ability cannot change in any meaningful way, no matter what we do. For these people, the traits we have are the traits we were born with, and the traits that we'll die with too. Success for these people is nothing more than the affirmation of their inherent intelligence, the abilities they were granted by an accident of biology or birth. She shows how this comes out in our everyday vernacular – 'I am not a numbers person', 'I can't draw' etc. Those of us with a 'growth mind-set', meanwhile, see the world differently. To these people, our character traits, our intelligence, our abilities – even such fundamental things as our confidence, our capacity to love, our capacity to learn itself – are acquired skills. Rather than thinking that our abilities are the result of some innate gift we've been given, people with a growth mind-set accept that we can change and grow across our lives, becoming more courageous, more intelligent, more calm or studious, by practise.

If this sounds straightforward, hold tight – it's about to get interesting. Dweck's research focused on school students and how their mind-sets influenced their future prosperity. Perhaps it's predictable that those who were found to have growth mind-sets went on to enjoy greater success in later life. But what startled Dweck – and what feels so much less predictable – was that it didn't matter whether neuroscientists agreed that intelligence genuinely was malleable or not; what mattered in determining someone's future prosperity was whether they themselves *believed* in its malleability. Students who made an active decision to believe they could change, develop and grow – that they weren't held back by immutable laws of nature – were, on average, more prosperous, settled and happy in later life. Having a growth mind-set, it turned out, was an active choice any one of us can make. Growth mind-set is not something you *have*; it's something that you choose.

In the world of STRETCHONOMICS, Dweck's thinking has a clear message.[7] People with a fixed mind-set find it difficult to stretch. For them, to fail at something is the same as it being confirmed that they're naturally unable, naturally unintelligent, and thereby no good. They often tend to blame failure on external factors, whilst claiming success as very much their own. This mind-set makes the Stretch Zone a frightening place – because the Stretch Zone is a place where failure is an everyday, galvanising part of life.

Meanwhile, those of us who choose instead to have growth mind-sets are able to recognise failure for what it is: an agent of change. People who adopt growth mind-sets don't see failure as evidence of unintelligence but as a heartening springboard for growth. They know that character, competence, intelligence and everything else in life is out there, waiting to be developed or acquired. For them, the Stretch Zone is an inviting place, and setting TARGETS – realistic ones, yes, but on occasion ones that might be beyond them – is central to both progress and also success – however one chooses to define it.

Having a fixed mind-set has a negative impact on TARGET setting. Thinking 'I'm not a long-distance' runner would hold you back from setting an ambitious target for an upcoming race. This limits the individual's potential – it prevents them from ever setting a stretch TARGET, because the failures they expect along the way will only serve to reinforce the negative beliefs they hold about themselves. On the other hand, an individual who makes an active choice to adopt a growth mind-set will embrace a challenge, seeing it as a way of bettering themselves, not as a threat to their tightly-held sense of self. This is exactly the situation Sir Mo Farah found himself in, when tasked with completing his first ever marathon. Was he afraid of a new challenge because failure in it would impact the sense he had of himself or his wider reputation or legacy as an athlete? Or was he ready for the challenge, knowing that – whether he succeeded or failed – he'd won in the long-term, just by the simple act of trying?

We see examples of the differences between a fixed and growth mind-set almost everywhere we look. The movie *Talledaga Nights* is perhaps an unusual source of inspiration in a book like this but it's a mental image we hold dear. In the film, the main character, NASCAR superstar Ricky Bobby (played by Will Ferrell), is driven by this simple belief: 'If you ain't first, you're last!'. As the plot develops, Ricky Bobby learns that his (fixed) mind-set is holding him back from regaining his legendary status and courage, which he lost after a disastrous crash. It is only when Ricky Bobby confronts his good-for-nothing drunken father that he understands his plight. In the movie, the exchange goes like this:

Ricky Bobby: 'Dad, you always told me, if you ain't first, you're last!'
Father Bobby: 'That doesn't make any sense at all, Son . . . You can be second, third, fourth . . . Hell, you can even be fifth!'

On his road back to success, with his father as his mentor, he undergoes a classic sports movie transformational training regime. The key moment (at least for us) is when his father brings the metaphor to life by locking a wild cougar in a car and forcing his son to get in with it. It is by trying to get into the car with the cougar that Ricky Bobby leaves his fixed mind-set behind and embraces the growth mind-set. Winning and losing is no longer all or nothing and, consequently, Ricky Bobby goes on to defeat his flamboyant French nemesis. We all have our own 'cougars in the car', so it requires a certain amount of COURAGE to set the right target (more of which later), and to be prepared to fail.

We are not suggesting for a second that the makers of *Talladega Nights* were inspired by Dr Dweck's book, or even that there is any hard link at all between them. But the lesson we can derive from this, along with Sir Mo Farah and Carole Dweck herself, cannot be clearer: those of us who adopt a growth mind-set will embrace the potential of the Stretch Zone so much more fully. By facing the cougar in the car, we can ultimately improve our chances of success.

This is as true for organisations as it is individuals. Organisations in which growth mind-sets are endemic are better poised to rise to a stretching goal. They'll react positively to a stretch, embracing it as an opportunity to grow – rather than as a threat to be avoided. Organisations that measure their successes solely via outcomes – revenue raised, profits increased, value of shares – have fixed mind-sets in which success and failure are binary – or opposites – while organisations with growth mind-sets invest and learn from failures. AG Lafley is a two-time CEO of consumer goods giant Procter & Gamble and is very open in his book *Gamechangers* about his ten most expensive failures. One of us can claim to have worked closely on several of these projects and witnessed first hand how P&G defined failure differently to others, resulting in a lack of stigma or shame. When the plug was pulled on a failed launch, there was always a celebration and sharing of the learning that had been achieved to ensure that the lessons were learned and never repeated by any part of the organisation. This would be impossible in an organisation with a fixed mind-set.

Organisations which value learning and improving are, in our experience, better poised to grow and succeed and ultimately reap the financial rewards. For these organisations, financial rewards are the natural result of valuing people and fostering the growth mind-set. And, just like with individuals, the beautiful thing is that an organisation gets to *choose*. That's exactly what Microsoft's CEO, Satya Nadella, did in 2017 when he set himself the task of instilling the growth mind-set across the whole of the Microsoft organisation. Stretch goals have always been vital to Microsoft. One of their earliest – to put a computer running the Microsoft operating system in every home – is responsible for laying the foundations of the computer age itself. But Nadella realised that, to make stretch goals achievable rather than intimidating, he would need to convince Microsoft of the importance of the growth mind-set.

That's exactly what he did. 'We fundamentally believe,' he told them in his 2017 address, 'that we need a culture founded in a growth mind-set. It starts with a belief that everyone can grow and develop; that potential is nurtured, not predetermined; and that anyone can change their mind-set... We need to be always learning and insatiably curious. We need to be willing to lean in to uncertainty, take risks and move quickly when we make mistakes, recognizing that failure happens along the way to mastery. And we need to be open to the ideas of others, where the success of others does not diminish our own.'

It's a sentiment which is increasingly common from companies as diverse as Adidas, GE and Unilever as well as anyone interested in Stretch.

Everyone Can Stretch More Than They Think

We said it at the start and it's worth saying it again: setting targets might look easy, but the fact is it's anything but. Being able to identify a target that is ambitious enough to make you stretch, not too ambitious to demotivate, and yet still the right level to challenge, inspire and provoke new, appropriate behaviours, is a fine balance. Much of our work has been to help companies identify the TARGET that is right for them by taking into account their levels of ambition, the RESOURCES (time, money, talent) they have at hand and the behaviours they exhibit on a day to day basis (COURAGE and HUNGER).

But there's a secret we've observed through many years of Stretchonomics that suggests that targets that seem out of reach might actually be within our grasp. It's called the 40% rule.

Jesse Itzler, a one-time MTV rapper turned highly successful businessman (and long-distance runner), wrote a fascinating book based on a chance meeting he had with a Navy SEAL –

Living with a SEAL. Itzler was part of a six-person relay team running a 100-mile race in San Diego when he spotted David Goggins, the aforementioned retired Navy SEAL, running the entire race alone. Itzler was fascinated and kept an eye on Goggins throughout. Three quarters of the way into the race, the SEAL had broken all the small bones in his feet, damaged his kidney through sheer endurance – and yet still found it within himself to finish the race. Itzler was hooked and asked him what on earth compelled him to do this, and how he had developed the capability. What the SEAL said to him is fascinating. 'When your mind is telling you you're done,' the SEAL told him, 'you're really only 40% done.' It's the reason, the SEAL explained, why, even though many people hit a physical 'wall' in the latter stages of a marathon (the wall is a rather unpleasant point where the body and brain starts to suffer from depletion of a key carbohydrate called glycogen), 99% of people who enter a marathon still cling on to finish the race. 'When we think we're done, we're not nearly done.' We love that thought!

Itzler's book chronicles what happened when he invited this Navy SEAL to live with him for a month. It didn't take long before Itzler was brutally introduced to the realities of the 40% rule. On their first morning together, the SEAL instructed him to do 100 pull-ups. For Itzler this task seemed an impossibility. He managed 8, but the SEAL didn't let him give up. After a 30-second break, Itzler did 6 more pull-ups, took another break and, after that, found the strength to do 4 more. Then, one by one – with a brief respite between each – Itzler fought his way to a full 100. It was a moment of epiphany. Until that day Itzler hadn't thought such a thing was possible. But it revolutionised the way he thought about himself, what his potential for growth was. The truth is: everyone has more in them that they might think. And if you can hold onto this when you think about your TARGETs, you might just stretch to places you'd never thought possible.

The 40% rule doesn't just have Goggins and Itzler on its side. The science behind the rule is also clear that, though our minds and bodies aren't actually limitless, most of us can revise our limits dramatically upwards. A 2008 study found that subjects who were given a placebo but told it was caffeine were able to lift significantly more weight than another group who were actually given caffeine.[8.] The secret? Well, the mere belief that their bodies might be stimulated to do better *made* those bodies do better.

The 40% rule is not there to force us to perform at more than twice our original capacity. It's not asking us to achieve 100%. But it is there to show us that our limits are the ones we set for ourselves; that sometimes what we perceive as our boundaries are just lines we have imagined, based on past experience and outside influence; that, more often than not, we sell ourselves short by assuming we can't do something, can't take that extra step, can't run an extra mile – when the truth is there is much unlocked potential in all of us. As Itzler himself says, we all have a 'reserve tank' that we barely tap into. The reason? 'People stick to what's comfortable. But, when you leave that zone, that's where you find true results and really see what you are capable of… When you're frustrated, when you're done, when you hit a road block, you have so much more left in you.' All of us, whether we're embarking on our first Stretch or our thousandth, can benefit from the wisdom of those words. We don't need to kill ourselves and work every single hour under the sun to smash through the 40% rule. A little extra spirit, the courage to go back and try again, even when we might think that we're drained, and – quite simply – the *belief* that we can do better than we've done before, is all it takes to reveal that we're capable of transforming our own limits. When we think we're done, we're not nearly done.

Targeting Your Target

Whenever you're setting out on a new Stretch, keep these simple reminders at the forefront of your mind:

1. Our TARGETS are the FUEL that keep us going. They should be fulfilling, uncomfortable, expressive and focused on learning.
2. Fulfilment is the definition of success. Benchmarking ourselves against others or being motivated purely by outward success – awards, bonuses and other financial imperatives – is never enough.
3. Stretch Goals can be problematic – but, used correctly, they're a fascinating way of pushing us further, to accomplish new things and to learn about ourselves.
4. Our targets must be dynamic. By constantly monitoring and assessing our targets, we can make the important adjustments that will continue to let us grow.
5. The growth mind-set is key to both individuals and organisations – and, what's more, we can all make the conscious decision to adopt it even if it means dealing with the cougar in the car.
6. Setbacks are inevitable; it's how you deal with them that matters.
7. Remember the 40% rule: when we think we're done, we're not nearly done.

CHAPTER 3: **RESOURCES**

- Exploring types of resource
- Why and how scarcity can be a good thing
- Making the most of what you have and the importance of making choices

With his SCOPE and TARGET decided, our marathon runner has locked down the parameters of his stretch ambition. But that's less than half of the Stretchonomics equation – because, if he's going to succeed in that ambition, he's going to have to match it with his stretch commitments. We go back to the balance between the things we want and the things we are prepared to do to achieve them. How does our runner *know* he'll be able to finish the race in his chosen time? How does he know he'll be able to get to race fitness before the marathon begins, and that his body will stand up to the pressures of the long-distance course? Only by making sure that his ambition is matched by his commitment will he find himself in the Stretch Zone, with the highest likelihood of success. Over the next chapters we'll be diving into the detail of the five Stretch dimensions that together make up our commitments: exploring the Resource, Techniques and Execution of a plan, along with the behaviours required to Stretch, our COURAGE and HUNGER. But first let's talk about our 'R; – RESOURCES.

What Are Resources?

In Stretchonomics, we think of RESOURCES in the broadest sense. And, whether we're at the head of a company looking to achieve greater things, or a wannabe marathon runner just setting out, the question of managing resources that always have limit is just as relevant.

Most aspects of Stretchonomics apply just as easily to individuals as they do companies, but when we think about RESOURCES it's helpful to separate the two. In business we think of resources as being one of four types:

1. **Physical Resources.** Have we enough equipment, enough buildings, enough workshop space to accomplish the goals we've set ourselves? Think of Physical Resources as the tangible things your company needs to thrive: the space, raw materials and infrastructure upon which almost every business exists.

2. **Intellectual Resources.** Are our brands, patents, intellectual property (IP) correct and up-to-date? Do we have enough knowledge in a particular area to compete and succeed? These types of resources might be intangible but they often take a great deal of time and expenditure to develop and can drive competitive advantage. Tech unicorns like Airbnb don't rely on physical assets like factories or large numbers of people but on the software and algorithms they've created and continually improve. Patentable ideas and software are more and more valuable in the digital age. In fact, the number of patents filed by tech giant Google grew by 170% between 2011 and 2012, and Apple's patents also exploded exponentially. Customer knowledge, access to customers, and – ever more pertinent in the age we live in – data collated on customers' likes, dislikes and attitudes, all constitute a form of intellectual resource it's critical to cultivate.

3. **Human Resources.** Do we have the right number of employees, skills mix, experience, partners, and time to accomplish what we've set out to do? The people inside your organisation are often an overlooked resource – and yet, when somebody leaves, we often feel there's a void that needs to be filled. Across time,

we invest in developing people and bringing their skill-sets into our businesses. Beyond traditional metrics, it's worth considering the knowledge and experience of the people in the business and the time they have to deploy this on the things which matter, rather than the short-term tyranny of email demands.

4. **Financial Resources.** Do we have enough money to invest in the things we need to, in order to achieve the target? Are there appropriate levels of accessible cash and credit to smooth the way for our enterprise to succeed? Capital to invest in new infrastructure and inventory in support of a stretch is vital, but so too are the financial resources that can keep us afloat in times of scarcity. How we manage our financial resources is often the difference between the life and death of a company. In business, the balance sheet is often used as a metric of success but sharp management of resources is a key enabler of this.

For our marathon runner or any other individuals embarking upon a personal stretch ambition, resources should be defined similarly but slightly differently. As an individual we think of resources as belonging to three broad types:

1. **Money.** We're back to financials again. Do we have enough financial resources to chase our target? Does our marathon runner have the cash he needs to invest in new equipment, the services of a personal trainer… or might it be that, with enough money in the bank, he can take a few mornings a week off work, and therefore give himself more time? This sort of financial 'breathing space' is often critical to the early stage entrepreneur.

2. **Time.** How much time does our marathon runner have for training? There are only twenty-four hours in a day and significant chunks of this have to be given over to work, to family, to whatever other commitments we've made in our lives.

We can't stretch time, but we can – as we'll see – use it more effectively. Here, as elsewhere, making good choices is key to getting more from the same resource.

3. **Energy.** It might be difficult to quantify how much energy we have in our lives, but we definitely know when we don't have it. As individuals, we are often torn in a dozen different directions as the demands of family, friends, work and health take their toll. Have we enough emotional space and energy to succeed? Are we in good physical shape, and is our motivation as strong as it must be to go to the places we've planned?

Whether you're stretching as a business or an individual, think of your resources as assets which could and should be used in the pursuit of your target. Often they are limited by factors beyond your control. Individuals and businesses only have access to so much money. There are only twenty-four hours in a day. Businesses can only realistically sustain a certain head-count and skills mix, and individuals can only invest so much emotional energy into their pursuits before something else has to give. Careful management and stretching of these resources is a critical factor in any stretch – and getting it right is all down to understanding the complexity of the relationship between Scarcity and Choice.

Scarcity Is The Mother Of Invention

It might seem natural to think of resources as the magical elixir that will guarantee your business or personal success. With enough money in the bank, you might think, a company could accomplish anything. And there are certainly plenty of high profile examples where companies, people and other groups rich in resources – especially financial – have had stratospheric successes. Just think of Team GB and their successes at both the London 2012 Olympics and, later, the 2016 Olympics in Rio de Janeiro. Intangible factors like team spirit, home advantage and 'talent' certainly played their part in the number of medals Team GB won at these events, but scratch beneath the surface and the role the £350m of funding directed at elite sport in the United Kingdom across the four years preceding the games is difficult to ignore. One statistician calculated that every gold medal that Team GB won in 2016 came with a price tag of £5.5m, most of it coming from National Lottery grants. The investment in athletics infrastructure, coaching and people paid off in a spectacular way. And the same can be seen across other professional sports. In *Soccernomics*, Simon Kuper and Stefan Szymanski showed how the wage bills of professional football players can drive the success of a club. Across the game, the correlation between the wages bill of a team is a reliable indicator for their long-term success over a season. Just ask any Arsenal fan!

It's interesting to note that, when they launched the first iPad, Apple were investing 30% of their turnover in Research and Development whilst most FTSE 100 companies struggle to invest 5%. But if it seems self-evident that more resources equals more success, it's time to think again. Anyone who has trained for a 5k run, a 10k run, or even just a jog around the block, will tell you that their running performance is not necessarily improved by simply putting more and more training in. Studies have shown that the weekly mileage a runner puts into his sport is not, in itself, a good predictor of how they will perform in a race – and, in fact, lower mileage runners often surpass higher mileage runners when it comes to marathons, half-marathons and other long-distance events.[9.] Many of the most successful innovations of recent times have come from those with limited resources – just think of the current boom in start-ups.

There's a mystery here, and its answer boils down to 'Scarcity' and 'Choice' – the twin horns of the resource dilemma.

Scarcity and choice are, together, the foundation stones of economics and most economic theory. In fact, without them, there'd be no study of economics of all. When we talk of scarcity, what we mean is that the resources of the world, or our particular part of it, are always limited – while our *wants*, the things the consumer desires, have no upper limit at all. We could want everything in existence and more, but never be able to get it – because the resources that might satisfy us simply aren't there in enough abundance to do so. What this means, in practise, is that we – as customers, as individuals, as businesses large and small – have to make *choices*. Consider the office worker who, popping out for his lunch with only £5 in his hand, has to decide whether to go to the fast food joint over the road or the delicatessen further down the street. Perhaps he *wants* both – but he can't have them, because he's only got a single £5 note. His resources are limited so he must choose. Or consider the software start up who wants to grow their business – they need more users requiring marketing and sales investment, but to handle more users they need to upgrade their systems. With limited cash in the bank they can't do both, so they must choose. You can take this into daily life too – and, in fact, we're all doing this every day. You're doing it now. Your time is a finite resource. You can either sit here reading this book or go out for a run. You can't do both. The study of economics is the study of how scarcity and choice interact. How do we use our limited resources to satisfy our unlimited wants and needs?

Why doesn't more resource automatically equal more success – more productivity, better results, more instant income? Well, in Stretchonomics terms, what it means is this: too much resource can actually push us out of our Stretch Zones. When we have too many resources at hand, the result can be that we lose focus or even develop a kind of laziness that inhibits our performance. In short: with too many resources, our mind-set changes. When we have surplus cash, we might be tempted to spend more than we need to. When we have too much time, we might squander it pursuing unnecessary avenues, not getting things done as efficiently and time-sensitively as we might. And in running, there's strong evidence to show that actively limiting resources like time can lead to improved fitness. High intensity interval training – in which people go through specific exercises at maximum intensity for only short bursts of time – is based on this exact precept. In business, recent studies by the Office of National Statistics in the UK have shown how self-employed and small and medium-sized businesses (SMEs) are driving and supporting productivity of the entire economy – thanks to lower sickness rates and better return on investments than larger companies. They typically don't have much resource to spare, so they have to maximise the resources they do have.

Too much resource can cause a lack of focus, an unhelpful level of comfort, even laziness that is detrimental to performance. We've seen this first-hand. When we were engaged to review the innovation performance of a top 10 FTSE company, we researched and analysed performance across the major business units, each of which was based in a different part of the world. What we found was that, once we had factored out wider macro economic factors, the most resource-constrained business unit was actually performing best in terms of innovation return on investment. But how could that be? How is it possible that the best-resourced regional team were less successful than the least? Well, it turns out that this is far from being an exception. These business units, fully resourced, had become internally focussed, obsessed by due process, exploring the intellectually interesting rather than the commercially expedient. The underfunded, meanwhile. had to 'innovate or die' – they simply couldn't work on many ideas and the ones they did work on *had* to succeed. They had started working and thinking like a much smaller company – they had made choices around where and how to invest financially and in terms of their people. Interestingly, they had been especially good at spending time on the important things and not necessarily the urgent things!

The mind-set of a business rich in resources can too often lead to a type of self importance – 'I have more resources than my competitors, and this makes me powerful' – when, in fact, all the surplus of resources is doing is lulling them into a false sense of superiority. Resource-surplus firms invest heavily in new technologies and research and development, but this doesn't guarantee elevated results; especially if they don't match it with investing in their employees and the infrastructure needed to leverage those new innovations to market, or support the roll out of the new product. Often, resource heavy companies focus on creating new things more than pushing the things they have in the market, and thus any extra expenditure in R&D can be lost.

In contrast, firms with fewer resources are forced to adopt different approaches. Being constrained actually drives the creativity and fleet-footedness of these firms. Perhaps they have to conquer a niche market, focus more on core-competencies, or find ways to do more with less. It may feel strange to speak of global retail and technology giant Amazon in these terms – but, at its inception, Amazon was a tiny company with very few resources at all. By focusing on what was then a niche market, online bookselling, Amazon's founder Jeff Bezos was able to rapidly grow the company – a story that begins in the company founder's garage and ends in sub-orbital spaceflight, asteroid mining, and all the other bold ventures the company is making today.

Nobody has proved the power of innovating in a constrained space better than the Indian Space Research Organisation. (As an aside, India has led the way in pioneering a whole new school of innovation thought, that of Jugaad innovation or Frugal innovation, terms captured and explored originally in the writings of Navi Radjou, Jaideep Prabhu and Simone Ahuja.) Space travel and exploration, as you might expect, is an expensive pursuit. And yet, in 2014, the ISRO was able to send their satellite, the Mangaalayan Mars, to the Red Planet at a cost of only $75m – while

NASA's own Mars mission, launched only days later, cost almost 9 times as much, at $671m. To put this in context: the ISRO's Mars mission cost less than three quarters the money that Hollywood spent making *Gravity*, the movie about two astronauts going into orbit. Or think of it another way: getting to Mars cost the ISRO less per km than a rickshaw journey around Bangalore. Even more impressively, in 2016 they were able to launch the last of its Earthbound satellites at a complete cost of $350m – less than the extra capital the European Space Agency had to invest in their Galileo programme when it ran over budget. Time and again, the IRSO has shown that, although they don't have the depth of resources of their international counterparts, it doesn't put limits on them going to the stars.

How have they done this? Well, in a populous yet resource-starved nation like India, many sectors of the technology industry have been forced to look for cheaper, innovative alternatives to those used in richer countries, where a little money can take the place of hard graft and effort. It's no surprise that India has built the world's cheapest car, costing just $2,500, or the world's cheapest tablet computer, costing only $49. The space industry is no different. As the organisation's chairman, K Radhakrishnan says, 'Ours is a contrasting, inexpensive and innovative approach to a very complex mission.' Central to this is the art of re-using old technologies. Organisations like NASA might spend 5 or 6 years building new systems from scratch but, with more modest budgets and tighter time-frames – deliberately chosen to keep costs down – the ISRO has looked to other sectors and incorporated their knowledge and technologies into its own. Their launch vehicle was first developed in the late 1970s and augmented several times since; their altitude and other tracking systems are developed from technologies already present, retrofitted to their own projects. Their system means that they don't need to tailor make everything for each mission – so what was used on one mission can easily be replicated for another, dramatically cutting down their need for R&D. And what's more, they keep things local. Just like your local butchers and greengrocers, championing the cause of local farmers, the ISRO use purely Indian contractors to build their hardware locally. This is in stark contrast to NAA or the ESA, who pay exorbitant sums for old Soviet rockets and launch capabilities, rather than building their own.

So, if you don't have enormous resources – if your money is tight, your space too small, the demands on your time almost overbearing – it doesn't necessarily mean that there are limits being put on your potential success. Having tight resources might actually expose you to opportunities you might otherwise have overlooked – opportunities for innovation, for standing out, for doing things in a different way, and for exploiting every little opportunity that comes your way. Like the Indian Space Agency, scarcity might well describe the contents of your bank account, your warehouses, or the number of staff you have at your disposal – but, with the appropriate mind-set, it might actually be an advantage. Scarcity can truly be the mother of invention.

It's Not Just You Who Can Stretch. So Can Your Resources!

Not all of us have access to the kinds of venture capital or start-up funding that can help accelerate the launch a successful business. Not all of us have the capacity to set aside all of the other important things in our lives and dedicate 100% of our time and energy into a single endeavour. Life doesn't work like that and we shouldn't pretend that it does. But if scarcity is the mother of invention, how can we all find ways to make what resources we have, work harder for us.

The good news is that companies and other organisations with little start-up funding have had tremendous (and sometimes unexpected) success. American Football is a sport once confined to the shores of North America – but, in recent years, it has flourished across Europe. Despite having so little funding, teams like Milan's

Milano Seamen (you couldn't make it up!), the *Basel Gladiators*,
Lisbon's *Navigators* and the *London Warriors* are demonstrating consistently high levels of performance that belie their lack of tangible
resources. How can it be that a sport so under-funded can flourish?
Well, a closer look reveals that, although tangible resources such as
money to spend on importing players from around the world, are of
course important, the success of a team is in part driven by how the
team works together, the tactics it employs, and the chemistry that
can bond a group of players. By smart management of resources,
Europe's American Football teams have been able to get past the
stumbling blocks that may otherwise have held them back. They
have shown that having *less* doesn't hold back our ambition. Rather,
it can actually make us more ambitious, more determined to succeed
by getting the best out of what we have.

There's a name for this. The concept of doing more with fewer
resources is known as 'Resource Leverage' and it incorporates five
distinct ways in which resources can be stretched.[10.]

1. **Time Focus.** You don't have to be running a multinational
   corporation of 50,000 staff members to know the problems that
   can crop up if everyone isn't focused on the same goal. Even a
   company of three or four people or a team of 11 footballers can
   be deeply inefficient if its members aren't all pulling together.
   When different people have conflicting goals, it undermines focus,
   spreads resources too thinly and makes everything less efficient.
   For this reason, entrepreneurs are generally much better at
   focusing resources than big companies. They have focus because,
   for them, there is no Plan B... and nor is there any money!

   Focus matters for the big things as well as the small. Tony
   Schwartz might be more famous in his role as the ghost-writer
   of Donald Trump's *The Art of the Deal*, but in his career as
   business theorist and motivational speaker he's focused on the
   tricks we can all use to get the best out of our energy and time.

Schwartz is not alone in thinking there's a problem in time-management in the era of email and constant communication. A study by the University of British Columbia showed that the average person checks their smartphone 151 times a day.[11.] For Schwartz, checking email might give us the impression that we're busy – it engages the part of the brain that fuels a sense of accomplishment – but it means we're rarely busy with the *right things*. We're concentrating on 'urgent' things – an email flashing in the corner of our screens, the demands being made for our attention by somebody else – rather than the 'important' things, the things that will ultimately add most value to what we do. Even more problematically, checking our email regularly fragments our time – and time is one of our most valuable resources. Every time we check email we break off from the job in hand and, when we return to it, have to re-engage with it, losing yet more time while we work ourselves back into a groove. This lost time is a cost – and, if we're doing it a multitude of times a day, the cost soon stacks up. For what it's worth, Schwartz's answer is to begin each day focusing intensely for 90 minutes on an important task, without any interruptions from phone, email, or guests. For 90 minutes, studies show, the human body can concentrate intensely – but, at the 90 minute mark, the body reaches a kind of nadir at which the intensity of focus naturally starts to dwindle.[12.] Schwartz believes the key to stretching the resources of time and energy lies in resisting the false gratification of email and smartphone checking and instead committing to short bursts of intense, uninterrupted concentration.

2. **Accumulated Experience.** Resources are not only tangible. One of our most important resources is *experience*, something that we're accumulating that every day. Yet, some of us are better than others at getting the best out of our experiences. Companies who are 'learning organisations' are those who understand this and

look to actively grow and manage experience in the same way many look to do so with financial resource on the balance sheet or product in the supply chain. Just like Microsoft and their growth mind-set from the previous chapter, they recognise that knowledge itself is a resource and invest in it accordingly. There couldn't be a better example than online streaming service Netflix. Netflix's prime business is in making sure they not only attract new customers but retain the customers they already have – and the key to them doing this is that they constantly assess their own performance, their consumers' behaviour and ways the quality of the customer experience can be improved. Making learning and adapting a prime part of your business is critical – but simply being a learning organisation is never enough; instead, you have to be capable of learning more efficiently than your competitors. For anyone interested in learning and business culture, it is worth looking online for Netflix's 'Reference Guide on our Freedom & Responsibility Culture', an internal document which has made its way into the public domain – potentially deliberately! Netflix has built a culture around wanting to work with people who embody values such as curiosity, honesty, communication and passion. Values are part of the challenge but knowledge and experience is another, and companies who resist the temptation to only hire people in the early stages of their careers often have an advantage. 'Young heads' are often characterised as having more courage, more hunger, more get-up-and-go about them, but we overlook 'old heads', those with their accumulated knowledge and experience at our peril. 'Old heads' bring knowledge and experience to a company, and that's a resource we can't develop any other way.

3. **De-Siloing.** Possessing resources is only one part of a more complex puzzle. We can possess all the resources in the world, but unless we use those resources properly we won't accomplish everything – and one of the most significant hindrances to this

is what author Gillian Tett has called the 'Silo Effect'.[13.] Possessing resources is different from applying those resources to advantageous effect and, in modern companies, resources are often so compartmentalized that their impact on each other are greatly reduced. Tett shows that, whilst sometimes silos can be useful – such as allowing big companies to recruit and manage groups of specialists – they can become insular and distinct from the rest of the organisation and its Targets and Scope. As a result, opportunities are missed, inefficiencies are created and the resources that might in theory be available are squandered. And that's exactly what happened to Sony in the 1990s and early 21st century. Sony had become so vast and successful that its leadership decided to split the company into a number of smaller entities to improve efficiency. In the short term, it worked – the reorganisation sent profits into the stratosphere – but when a culture of internal competition kicked in, with the new 'silos' stopping working together as closely as they once had, Sony found themselves in trouble. So much so that, with the advent of digital music, they weren't able to react swiftly enough and were quickly eclipsed by the advent of Apple and its era-defining iTunes store. Would this have happened if Sony wasn't an organisation built out of many different silos? We see silos as a real inhibitor in our innovation work because they create two challenges. Firstly, they foster a strong internal focus. A recent study we conducted amongst executives tasked with managing innovation showed that the majority of their time was spent not on shaping the idea but 'managing stakeholders' via internal meetings and due process. The second challenge caused by silos is that to grow a business or make an innovation successful, the experts assembled by the company must work together. A new product needs the support and input of sales, marketing, finance, supply, distribution, legal and more to get out of the door and be grown to scale.

Combining resources and working together is a critical skill to acquire, and that can only really happen with an open, communicative organisation – as the Netflix values suggest – rather than one where walls have been built up between departments, leading to mistrust and the senior management becoming more of a focus than the real customers who pay everyone's salaries. By combining different types of resource we can actually multiply the value of them, and avoid the silo effect. An interesting if unglamorous example of this is how household goods manufacturer Procter & Gamble (Justin's alma mater) developed their teeth whitening product, Crest Whitestrips. P&G are a vast company with many different divisions producing many different products, but the communication across the company allowed them to combine knowledge from their paper products division, bleach technology from their fabric products and the glue from another application to produce a completely new product. And this is something P&G have prided themselves on: the ability to produce disruptive new ideas by using seemingly disparate, but actually complimentary, parts of their business. As their Chief Technology Officer, Bruce Brown has said, 'The magic in a big company is how to create space for connections.' Connectivity, along with trust and honesty, lies at the heart of silo-killing, so much so that at Google HQ, lunch queues are created to drive interaction.

4. **Asset Maximising - or Making the Most of What You Have.** Conservation isn't just for the environment. It's for all aspects of life – and business is no different. Think about recycling in terms of your business. Using the same resource in as many ways as possible – like Sharp does, exploiting its expertise in liquid-crystal-display for use in calculators, mini-TVs, laptop computers and many other products – is only one of the ways recycling can work. Honda has recycled its engine-related innovations for use in motorcycles, cars, outboard motors,

generators and garden tractors – but don't overlook the fact that brands can be recycled too. Remember Stella Artois launching a cider in 2011? Well, 'recycling' the brand-name of their well-known lager helped give this new product instant market presence and momentum from day one. One can imagine the meetings at Stella HQ and the furious debate about whether a beer company should even launch a cider and, if it did, whether it should be launched under the Stella name or given a new brand name of its own.

There are other ways to conserve the resources you have at hand as well. If you're entering a market where bigger companies dominate, you might think it a battle not worth fighting – and, indeed, attempting to match a larger competitor strength-for-strength is a waste of resources that might better be spent elsewhere. But… what can you do to disrupt the natural state of a market? Are there weak spots where you might enter a market and change it from the inside, instead of wasting resource fronting up to better provisioned players? This is exactly what Apple did with the launch of their iconic product, the iPhone. At the time of its launch, Nokia was the biggest seller of mobile phone hand-sets in the world – but by entering the market by launching its smartphone, then a niche product that Nokia did not believe would be of interest to anyone other than in business, Apple transformed the landscape.

Finally, think about co-opting the resources of others as a way of making your own go further. Perhaps you and a potential competitor have a bigger enemy in common? Perhaps there's a way of working collectively to establish a new standard or develop a new technology, something that might diminish the bigger rival and open up opportunities for yourself? By co-opting the resources of others, can you extend your influence in your field? Budget airlines Ryanair and EasyJet have tradi-tionally seen the bigger airlines as competitors, but now they're exploring partnering with flag carriers by becoming feeders for long haul journeys. By co-opting each other's resources and standing united, both budget airlines have the capacity to extend their own reach. Increasingly we see a blurring between competition and co-operation – partnerships and joint ventures emerging where there is a clear fit between capabilities or resources, be they financial, geographic footprint, supply, distribution or sales.

5. **The Need for Speed.** In any business there's a time-lag between the expenditure we make to take products and services out to market and the financial return we receive, and this is yet another form of leverage. The quicker the turnaround, the better the use of resources. Think of 'speed' as a 'resource multiplier' – the faster we get our revenue back from the market, the more quickly we can use that revenue to get yet more products out there and make yet more revenue. A company that can increase its efficiency and turnaround its products twice as fast as its competitors will quickly outstrip them. It's this rudimentary arithmetic that explains the dominance of the Japanese auto-industry over the traditional American car manufacturers in the late 20th century. If a car manufacturer in Detroit takes 8 years to bring a new model to market and a car manufacturer in Japan introduces a new model every 4.5 years, it's easy to see how one company quickly overtakes the other. The Japanese firm not only recoups its investments more quickly, they also give customers more opportunities to switch their brand loyalties. It's this kind of disruptive practise that can transform a business landscape and technology is making this a scary reality for many asset heavy, slow moving, large companies.

In Stretchonomics, then, it's not only how much resource you have that matters; it's also the ability to leverage and apply it.

Making the Trade: The Dilemma of Choice

Scarcity is the first dilemma of resource management, but it goes hand-in-hand with the second: the dilemma of choice. Every time we make a resource decision – where should we spend our money, how should we use our time? – we're not only choosing what *to* do; we're choosing what *not* to do as well. Be warned, because this is the thing that, in our experience, we all struggle with the most: when we do one thing with our resources, we necessarily have to stop doing something else. Our resources might be stretchable, but they're not infinite. And it's in the choice between the two that stretches succeed or fail.

A few years back we contacted a man called Caspar Berry to help us on a project we were working on, looking at risk and investment in innovation. Caspar Berry isn't just an ex-professional poker player and regular face on late-night poker TV. He is a Cambridge economist, motivational speaker, business guru, and one of life's good guys who uses his experience at the high stakes Poker tables of Las Vegas as a metaphor to help people improve decision making. Caspar argues that every decision we make in life is just another form of 'investment decision'. In the same way that companies are constantly making choices about which projects, initiatives or businesses to back, individuals are constantly making decisions about how to spend our money, our time, our personal commitment and energy. For Berry, if you choose to invest in one thing, then you are consciously choosing *not* to invest in another. If you decide to invest time in training for your triathlon, you are choosing not to spend that time with your family, doing the gardening or whatever else may require your time or energy. Should you spend money on a holiday or on redecorating the house? To Berry, these are the same kind of 'investment decisions' as a company makes when deciding what projects to spend their limited budgets and team time on.

What Caspar Berry thinks of as 'investment decisions', economic theorists call 'trade-offs' – and trade-offs create opportunity costs, one of the most important concepts in economics. Whenever you make a trade-off, or a choice, the thing that you do not choose becomes your opportunity cost. You bought that bike? Then the day-trip to Paris that you didn't buy was the opportunity cost. Decided to work late last night? Your opportunity cost was a catch-up with friends over a beer.

Everything has an opportunity cost. If you just bought something, you could always have bought something else instead. This 'something else' might seem insignificant, but thinking about it and balancing it against the things we actually choose is one of the most important things we can do. Making a bad trade-off can be frustrating, a waste – or, at worst, catastrophic. That two months we spent researching markets in France when we might instead have been developing a stronger distribution system in our home market? That money we spent on a new warehouse instead of the new stock to fill it? The redundancy pay-out spent on a new flashy sports car instead of starting a new venture or paying the kids' tuition fees? Let the imagination run riot for a moment and you quickly start to see how disastrous a bad trade-off can be.

The ability to make sensible trade-offs is one of the most important in business and life. But how to make these decisions confidently? Opportunity costs can rarely be calculated – because they're less tangible and more complex to measure than the choices we've actually made. After all, in most cases, we can collect data and interrogate it for the choices we've made, but an opportunity cost is just a hypothetical and much more difficult to pin down. How could we ever measure, for instance, whether the triathlon runner was right to spend his or her final afternoon on a training run, rather than in the pool swimming?

But in Stretchonomics, we have some robust tools at our disposal. And by examining the way we make our decisions, we can make sure that, whatever trade-offs you're forced to make, the opportunity cost is as low as it can possibly be.

First, let's go back to our S and T. Having a clear SCOPE and TARGET is absolutely key in making the right trade-offs. Without a SCOPE and TARGET that are working in clear alignment, it becomes impossible to assign resources effectively. Committing resources to one thing over another must always be driven by *what* you want to achieve and *how*. When it comes time to make an investment decision – whether investing time, money or personal energy – go back to your SCOPE and TARGET first. Are they in alignment? Are they correct? If there's any doubt, think again.

Next, consider the question: how objective are you? There's little doubt that rational and objective decision making is critical to the success of every endeavour – and even more so when we have limited resources. In an ideal world we'd be able to base our decisions on complete knowledge; in the real world this is rarely available, but we must base our decisions on as complete a set of information as we can.

To be rational in our decision making, we have to be aware of the biases built into us all as humans. And what this means is that any resource investment decision we make is unlikely to be purely rational. By acknowledging this, we can mitigate the effect of the biases working their dark magic on us. Individuals, management teams and coaches all have emotional biases that subconsciously steer the choices we make. But the companies and individuals who make the best investment decisions and/or trade-offs are the ones who are most capable of resisting their behavioural biases and making decisions informed by the reality of a situation, not the emotion invested in it. Come with us, for a moment, into the world of behavioural economics, a topic recognised when Richard Thaler was awarded the Nobel Prize in 2017, and something we first came across a decade ago in the mysterious world of multi-million dollar oil deals in the Middle East (if we tell you, we'd have to kill you).

The first way to manage these biases is to understand them. Only then can we do something about it. These biases are wide and varied and common to us all. They are integral to how our brains manage information and deal with choice. Treat the below as a taster; there are hundreds of books on 'Behavioural Economics' which will satisfy those with a greater hunger:

(a) **Endowment Bias (or why 'jam today' beats 'jam tomorrow').** As human beings, we're programmed to value the things we have *now* more than the things we might have in the future. It's probably hard-wired into us. Back when we were hunter gatherers, having a stockpile of meat to eat *now* was much more important than the promise of more meat in days to come. But in business this very human failsafe can lead us to holding onto resources when, in fact, we would be better placed investing them and seeing them grow. Resisting this bias means knowing that there's a right time to invest resources, and it often comes earlier than we think. This is linked to…

(b) **Loss Aversion (or why we fear losing more than we love winning).** Ask yourself if you'd rather lose the £20 in your wallet or find a random £20 note. If we're being honest, most of us would answer the same – that we'd rather avoid a loss than make a gain. Richard Thaler showed that the fear of losing something doubly outweighs the prospect of winning the same amount. We call this 'loss aversion' and it's a behavioural bias that can make us reluctant to take risks. For one of our multinational clients, this is a deep-seated bias. As a consequence they find it very difficult to sacrifice even a small amount of existing business in order to free up resources to invest in bigger, new operations. Only by continually challenging this way of thinking can they make the most out of the resources they have.

(c) **The Break-Even Effect (or the rebound effect).** When we've hit a problematic patch in life, we often feel compelled to make up for it as quickly as possible. For an individual this might manifest as the manic desire to get back into a relationship after the collapse of a marriage, or in business it might mean that, when we've lost money, we jump too readily at any chance to make up our losses – even if that means us taking bigger risks than feel natural to us. Being aware of the bias can help us spot when we might be about to make a catastrophic and out-of-character investment decision. Managing this aspect of the 'tilt' (a run of bad form) is a challenge at the poker and boardroom table alike.

If the picture we're building up of investment decisions is proving complex then, fantastic, we're doing our job. The number of variables involved, the lack of complete information – and the im-possibility of knowing exactly what might have happened if we'd made another decision – means that we'll never get our investment decisions correct 100% of the time. And do you know what? That's fine. As long as we're focused on our S and T, making our resource decisions in the context of that, and being aware of the behavioural biases that might be influencing us, we'll be in a good place to start making good decisions.

In our experience, big corporations often find making resource trade-offs tough. Because they have more resources to spread around, they can often avoid making tough calls by hedging their bets – spreading resources across too many projects, rather than pursuing fewer opportunities in a more focused way, in effect expecting high stakes poker returns whilst playing a large number of small return slot machines. This often results in a sense of frustration that they are not getting big returns and hitting their Targets. There is a pretty immutable law in business that the greater the risk, the greater the return – and making lots of little, safe investments will generally not create a 'step-change' in performance. Conversely, the scarcity of resources experienced by many entrepreneurs compels them to be more considered and focused in their investment decisions. They have to make choices. They are forced to 'go big or go home' (with apologies to those with an aversion to macho bullshit). We'll investigate this more fully in our upcoming 'C' chapter, but the difference between the two is as simple as a little courage. It might be easier for a big company to spread its resources around, doing lots of little things in the hope of advancing their cause –after all, nobody got fired for *not* making a 'mistake', and perhaps some people's fear of losing prevents them from trying to win. But the more courageous alternative is to do a few things in a bigger, bolder way. Scarcity, in case we need to keep reminding you, can be the very thing that drives us to excel.

The Right Way To Resource

So what have we learnt about the value and nature of resources in achieving a stretch goal, in hitting our S and T?

1. The levels, type and focus of your resources need to be aligned to your SCOPE and TARGET. If not, expectations are unlikely to be met. There is some negotiation required.
2. Resources are a complex combination of time, money and energy. In digital times, time is often the most scarce of all. We must protect our time to focus on the important over the urgent.
3. Scarcity is the mother of invention: just because you're not resourced as well as others doesn't mean you can't stretch more fully. Lack of resource can be the very thing that drives us – it can be an advantage when up against the big guys.
4. Every investment decision we make has an opportunity cost. We need to understand this and do so in the context of our natural biases – the short cuts we all make which differentiate 'behavioural economics' (what we do in reality) from 'pure economics' (what we should do rationally, with perfect information).

5. We need to constantly navigate the twin challenges of scarcity and choice in order to maximise how effective our resources really are.

6. We can't play the slot machines and expect poker returns – if we are to hit big targets we will need to take some risks and commit. It is a simple equation of 'resource x risk = reward'.

CHAPTER 4: **EXECUTION**

- How poor ideas well executed beat great ones poorly executed
- Tackling the "out of the box thinking" myth
- The power of doing over thinking

Our marathon runner knows where he's going (Scope). He has a Target – and he's cleared out the time to train (the right Resource). Now it's into the detail of preparing and executing a plan. At this point, he is faced with two choices. Does he do it the way he's done it before – training for a marathon as if it's just his usual Sunday run (more of the same but longer distances), or does he strike out, and look to new ways of training to achieve his ambition?

The first route always feels safer – in any field. Our marathon runner knows what's involved in his usual Sunday morning run. If he were to take this tried-and-trusted approach, he'd know what to expect: what pains his body might go through, what time he might achieve. The second option, meanwhile, feels more risky. Perhaps it means training in a different way – training short times at higher intensity, cycling, or doing some weight training. It might mean thinking about yoga, thinking about recovery, diet, stretching or Pilates. In this chapter we will look at the route less travelled: what happens when, in search of stretch, we take the decision to be different. We will explore how the search for original thinking can impact how we chase down our Target. And, although this route might feel scary at first, although there might be greater potential for experiencing failures and making mistakes along the way – it might just have greater impact as well.

In the business and sports worlds there is a simple truth: it's not just what you do, but how you do it, that counts. Or, to put it another way, judging from our experiences in business a shit idea well executed beats a great idea badly executed every time. Without exception. In sport it is not whether you go to the gym but how you train when you get there. With this in mind, never trust anyone who makes a big deal about going to the gym but reads the newspaper in the café or on the exercise bike – you know who you are! In this chapter we will focus on how to go about looking for inspiration and identifying the original approaches which will work for us, given our Scope, Target and Resource. In the chapter which follows, TECHNIQUE, we'll dig into the detail of the skills and capabilities we'll need to make these a reality.

Beer we go

In 2016 it was estimated that there were 1,700 craft beer breweries in the UK, which represented an 8% rise in the number of breweries on the previous year. In an age where mass-produced beers are available at such low prices, it's remarkable that these new products, which are generally more expensive to make and buy, are booming – not just in USA and Europe but in Asia, Africa and beyond.

Craft beer is a big and growing industry, representing nearly 20% of the US market by value – and its share is well into double figures in the UK, in an overall flat and declining market. In the craft beer world, there is a tried-and-tested approach – name your brewery after the place where it's located, hire someone to create a traditional, authentic-looking label, brew up a nice and strong hoppy IPA to put in the bottle, and give the brew an odd name based on either word play (hats off to Peter CottonAle, Hoptimus Prime, Audrey Hopburn, Pure Hoppiness and Smooth Hoperator) or something a little more risqué (shame on you to Hoppy Ending, Sex Panther, Arrogant Bastard Ale or Big Cock Ale). Pick a route

– 'clever' or crude – and you are all set. But this is not the only approach and is certainly not a guarantee of success.

BrewDog took an entirely different approach, with very different outcomes. The company was founded in 2007 and ten years later a private equity deal valued the company at over £1bn. Along the way, the company overcame a limited marketing budget in a noisy market dominated by some of the world's biggest companies with, until recently, no institutional investment. How did they do it? Well, one of the keys to their success was 'Equity for Punks', a funding approach ahead of its time, which offered fans of the beer the opportunity to invest directly in the company and become part of the business. In ten years, over 60,000 people have invested nearly £50m in BrewDog – meaning that they have more fans who have put their hard-earned cash into the business, than the average mainstream lager brand has Twitter followers. Think of this another way: not only do they have the cash, they have 60,000 brand advocates as well, each of whom feels some loyalty and incentive to push the brand. In a world where we trust people more than brands, this is a powerful marketing force as well as a significant financial investment.

Beyond this, BrewDog have consistently created challenging and controversial content, which has cut through all the 'usual marketing noise' giving them a louder voice than their budgets might suggest. Based on a clear sense of purpose (Scope), they have consistently 'aimed to make other people as passionate about great craft beer as we are'. Other facets of their Execution range from driving a pink tank through the City of London to marking the launch of 'Equity for Punks' by creating £1800 bottles of beer sold inside stuffed squirrels and stoats, to calling Vladimir Putin out on LGBT issues by sending a limited edition beer to the Kremlin – and even creating the world's strongest beer. All are done with a consistent 'punk' attitude and tone of voice. Their own online channel BrewDog TV pushes much of the content they generate –

tackling everything from how the beers are made to celebrating their legendary Punk AGMs, which are more akin to a mini festival – 2017 saw 7000 people entertained by seven guest brewers, seven bands and 15 food stalls. In fact, BrewDog are as remarkable in how they operate – their EXECUTION – as the outcomes and the beer they brew. The difference between a niche IPA and one of the fastest growing beer brands in the world is not in the bottle, but everything outside of it.

The same goes for those of us looking to stretch ourselves outside the world of business. For millennials, the prospects of getting a decent job after school or university has, in many countries, seemed a bit bleak for some years. At least, that's what they and we are constantly told. There's no doubt that in a country (and world) which is constantly becoming more populated, busy and fast-moving, where technology ensures that business can be done at the speed of light and the economy changes at frightening speed, there is less certainty about the employment market than ever before – especially given, as we have seen in recent work, the rise of Artificial Intelligence. As a result, competition for jobs is fierce. This means that submitting a standard CV as an application may not be enough to get noticed. But a 2013 survey showed that some candidates are willing to go the extra mile, approach things differently – and secure themselves a job along the way.[14.] Instead of just sending in regular CVs, candidates are looking to differentiate themselves based not only on their achievements but how they engage with potential employers. Some have made films, invested in billboards outside a potential employer's office, sent messages in a bottle to recruiters, or repaired a piece of the company's equipment during a first interview. One recent story came from a friend who was being interviewed for an industry award – he actually proposed to his interviewer (only in jest and possibly because he just happened to have his soon to be deployed engagement ring in his pocket). Instead of accepting that there was only one approach to take, these candidates reinvented the rules and were rewarded for their efforts.

What lesson can we learn from this? Well, having the idea to create a new craft beer or to change jobs is not as important as *how* you go about doing it. BrewDog are not the only company attempting to build market share in the craft beer market, and the graduate who sent a message in a bottle to a recruiter is not the only young graduate out looking for a job. Others have exactly the same ambitions. When preparing for the marathon, *how* you train is as important as *how much* you train. What you do matters (arguably, now more than ever), but *how* you do it matters more.

New Ideas, Old Rope

Still think there's a straight line between the quality of an idea and outcome (in business or even in sport)? Well, think again. Over the years, we've seen time and time again that having an idea and success are two completely different things, and the studies we've conducted have made it clear that the difference between the success and failure of any particular project is *not* the idea itself. It's about the quality and creativity of execution, clear and simple. In business, a bad idea executed well or originally beats an amazing idea, poorly executed or without imagination every time – although, to be clear, it sure as hell helps if the idea is a good one.

Look around you and you'll see examples everywhere that you turn, from the biggest corporation to the smallest pop-up store.

Think about Apple. Perhaps you're reading this book on an app on your iPhone or iPad right now. Well, you might be lulled into thinking that Apple's huge successes (an understatement) have happened because of their ground-breaking technological advances – but you'd be wrong. The iPod was late to the burgeoning MP3 and MP4 market. The iPhone was not the first Smartphone with a large screen, or the first able to download and use a series of apps. Nor was the iPad the first tablet, or the Apple TV the first

Smart TV. Apple's success is not down to the idea – it's down to the originality of their execution (again, an understatement). What Apple did better than anyone else was to understand the importance of design, of usability and of making consumers hungry for their product, what they call their 'emotional touchpoints'. Think of the Apple experience online and in-store, through to the semi-religious experience of opening the box. How you experience and interact matters as much as what the product actually does. It's not just what you do, but how you do it.

Or think about Wayne Huizenga – the only man in history to have launched three (yes, three) Fortune 500 businesses. His businesses were each distinct, but they have two things in common. None of them were first to market, and all became massive.

Huizenga founded his first firm, a waste collection business, in Fort Lauderdale, Florida in the late 1960s. At the time, there were other players in the waste collection market and no issues surrounding them. Consumers were happy with what they had – but along came Wayne with a single garbage truck and, after much expansion and acquisitions (133, to be precise), he had created Waste Management, Inc, which became a Fortune 500 company and, in 1983, the largest waste disposal company in the US.

In 1987, Huizenga turned his attention to video rentals. After buying a handful of video rental stores in 1987, he rebranded them as Blockbuster Video, then expanded, bought some more – and by 1994 his business became the leading video rental store in the country, as well as another Fortune 500 company.

Third was a US-wide chain of used car dealerships, AutoNation, built the same way as Waste Management, Inc and Blockbuster Video, partly by opening his own operations and partly through acquisitions. It didn't take long for AutoNation to hit the Fortune 500. Wayne had completed his hat-trick, and today he is thought to be worth over $2.5 billion – a story of success on an incredible scale.

This level of success is astonishing, but what's even more fascinating thing is that Huizenga's business 'ideas' were not the key drivers of his success. All were established industries, and none of these ideas were new. All of them had been done before. The thing that made Huizenga stand out was how he executed his plans, the way in which he was able to grow, acquire, scale and organise. He saw something that was going on, something other people were already doing – and did it not only bigger and better but differently.

The world of technology gives us plenty of examples. Think back to the Christmas of 2007. Millions of Kindles were sold that Christmas – and, in fact, people in the publishing world called it the Kindle Christmas for exactly this reason (at the time there were many harbingers of doom suggesting the end of publishing). You'd be forgiven for thinking that this was the year when ebooks were first launched, but in fact you'd be wrong. The Kindle might have been the device to properly transform the way we buy and sell books, but the first ebook reader came out almost a decade before. The first ebook reader was, in fact, the Rocket eBook, which came out in 1998. Sony's Librie was launched in 2004 and its Read in 2006, a whole year before the first Kindle.

But the Kindle, backed by the might of Amazon itself, was the product that really brought ebooks and their readers into the mainstream. How can that be, if so many others had blazed trails with similar projects for almost a decade beforehand? Take this to heart, because this is a lesson even the best of us need to learn: not every idea has to be a new one. In fact, there are so few new ideas out there that, often, we can waste our energy and other resources in chasing them down, rather than thinking about how we can grow what we have, executing originally. Wayne Huzienga knew this instinctively; for him, there was no need to reinvent the business world – he simply pinpointed things that people needed, and executed those operations incredibly well. And this is a principle which is just as applicable to our personal lives as it is to our work.

In *Smartcuts: How Hackers, Innovators and Icons Accelerate Success,* Shane Snow looks at how and why businesses succeed or fail, and why some succeed more quickly than their competition.[15.] One of his points fascinates us above all others. According to Snow, the popular business logic that the first company to launch themselves – or a product – into a market has an advantage over the competition is flawed. Snow concluded that first movers had a 47% failure rate and that 'companies that took control of a product's market share after the first movers pioneered them had only an 8% failure rate'. He compared first movers to early American pioneers exploring vast new terrains, and fast followers to people who followed their trails. Rather than having to break new ground in a market, those who come behind find a landscape that's already ready for the sorts of things they provide. According to Snow, fast followers are successful because they concentrate on what is happening in the market, in the real world. They can focus their time on execution not creation, on differentiation rather than explanation. They do not spend time thinking about the 'what' but the 'how'.

Get Back In Your Box!

The Stretch Zone is a place where we can realise ambitions we might once have thought beyond us. But there is nothing more dangerous, in the world of Stretchonomics, than crossing that line between a realistic stretch, a genuine ambition, and the realm of being a fantasist, disconnected from the real world. Forgive us a quick business focused rant. One of our pet hates is the language that comes with the kind of innovation we do. You might have heard these sorts of phrases bandied about in other business books. Pet hates include nonsense such as 'Ideation', 'Brainstorming' or 'Mindshowering'. A couple of other terms stand out as not only confusing but also wrong: 'Blue sky thinking' and 'Thinking outside the box'. In Stretchonomics it's important to see these phrases for what they are, because implicit within them are some assumptions which we believe to be extremely misleading.

We spend much of our working lives with start-ups and big businesses looking for new ideas, around which they can grow their businesses. We find many of them preoccupied with 'thinking outside the box', seeking to free themselves of the restrictions of their current situations. In reality we believe that 'thinking outside the box' is a flawed approach for one simple reason: there's *always* a box. Real life has a habit of throwing restrictions at us. These restrictions can take many forms and vary from one project to the next. They might be restrictions imposed by the company you work for, or the market in which you're looking to operate. In your personal life, they might be restrictions of geography, family, or time. Thinking 'outside the box' detaches us from reality. It encourages the dreaded 'blue sky thinking' where we are allowed to think the unthinkable, to go beyond our current constraints. The issue is that whilst this is a pleasant way to spend an afternoon, pretty soon those constraints will bite you. Thinking 'inside the box' demands that we stretch ourselves – it is innovation in the real world. It is not to say we must not challenge ourselves or be creative, but it is to acknowledge that we do have borders; we might really be hemmed in. The challenge is: how do we think originally within our given circumstances? What creative solutions are there to our problems? What can we do to get the best out of what we have? When we're locked down, inside the box, we have to think more nimbly, be more flexible, find ways of utilising what's right in front of us to get what we want – we are much more balanced between the what and the how. Put simply, inside the box is where we have to be at our sharpest. Outside the box you might get to fantasise, but inside the box you get to *stretch*. The same is true for our marathon runner – 'thinking outside of the box' for new ways to train will not help him if he has not got the time, expertise (Resource) or is not sure what time he is trying to achieve (Target). Ignoring the constraints doesn't mean that they are not there. Understanding them can be liberating.

The authors of *Inside the Box: A Proven System of Creativity for Breakthrough Results* argue that creativity is not helped by the removing of limits.[16.] In an interview, the authors were asked about the weaknesses of 'thinking outside the box'. They said: 'Thinking outside the box is a complete myth. It is based on flawed research from the 1970s. Subsequent research shows that simply telling people to think outside the box does not improve their creative output. It sends people on cognitive wild goose chases. Thinking inside the box constrains the brain's options and regulates how it produces ideas. By constraining and channelling our brains, we make them work both harder and smarter to find creative solutions. Contrary to what most people believe, the best ideas are usually nearby. Thinking inside the box helps you find these novel and surprising innovations.'

Over the years we have had the opportunity to spend time with some extraordinary people, from Michelin-starred chefs, award-winning comedians, Hollywood film directors, sculptors, artists and authors, elite sportsmen and women who have broken world records and won World Cups, Olympians who have been to multiple games, to special forces soldiers, as well as CEOs and successful entrepreneurs. These encounters have led to us to having a similar conversation over and over again: how did they achieve what they did? What did it take to be the best in their line of work? How much was down to inherent talent and how much was due to hard graft? How much was about their ideas or views of the world and how much of their success was driven by how they went about things, the application of their original thinking?

You might expect to find stories of inspiration, moments of sudden brilliance, but – even amongst this elite company – the truth is much more prosaic. Rather than rhapsodize about moments of pure creativity, the light bulb moments, the 'out of the box' insights, all of these people describe their achievements as the product of hours, weeks and months of practice, of rigour and dedication, of application and a constant desire to improve and learn. Imagine the Michelin-starred chef, creating new dishes for his restaurant under some of the closest scrutiny in his industry. Does he sit back and wait for a moment of inspiration? Does he wait until suddenly he knows – as if by magic – what new combination of ingredients and cooking techniques will result in the dishes by which he's remembered? Or does he, as our chef did, spend five long months developing a single dish on his restaurant's menu, working through several hundred attempts and repeated tastings and trials with key customers, tweaking one ingredient at a time, tweaking it again, tweaking it a third, fourth, fifth, one hundredth time, before finally – *finally* – getting it right? The idea for the dish was the easy bit, the tricky part was the Execution, getting it right on the plate. Then there was the Hollywood art director we once spent some time with. He talked of working on a James Bond film, and instead of 'brainstorming' ideas, he spent hours going back through a lifetime's worth of journals for ideas and inspiration. There was no sitting around waiting for the light bulb of genius to switch on. Instead, it was just hours and hours of dedicated trawling through the archives, painstakingly piecing something together until he knew the look, feel, texture of a single cinematic frame. Again it is not the idea but the Execution. Think, too, of the comedian: does he create his work in the sudden flurry of imagination? Or is there a reason comedians refer to their work as a *craft*? Instead, comedians describe creativity as going through thousands of ideas, rejecting most immediately and then trying out a few in front of small audiences, rejecting more and refining the ones which looked like they might work, before they eventually end up with their relatively short show. Again it is not only the idea but the Execution. There is no shortcut to success; the idea is important but the Execution critical.

This is important for anybody practising Stretchonomics. When approaching a new problem, don't automatically think about stepping 'outside the box'. Rather, think about what defines the box. Words on a page. Images on a screen. Jokes told by a man or woman standing on a stage with a mic in their hand. On a wet afternoon in Hereford, a year ago, a man in mirrored sunglasses described to us his work as a Special Forces Soldier. He described it as 'either ordinary warfare in extraordinary circumstances or extraordinary warfare in ordinary circumstances'. It's not only a little bit cryptic and exciting but it's also true to the principles above. Even for the 'best of the best' there are constraints and rules. We are better off understanding the box rather than ignoring it. Instead of crushing ideas, which is the accepted wisdom, this should liberate us.

In Stretchonomics, we have three ways to help define exactly what our particular box is: SCOPE, TARGET and RESOURCES. Our SCOPE lays out the direction in which we want to stretch, our TARGET how deep and lasting our stretch will be, and our RESOURCES help us realise how we're going to get there. In Stretchonomics, this is our box. We have set it for ourselves. Operating inside our own box is the critical difference between pushing ourselves realistically, or stepping into the fantastical, the wild goose chase of 'out of the box' and 'blue sky thinking'.

Dr Dragos (so jealous of his name!) of Entrepreneur magazine said it as clearly as anyone can: 'Creativity demands boxes... All of us, no matter where we're coming from, have boxes, have limitations. Maybe you have little kids you have to take care of, maybe you have older parents you have to take care of... your health, your age. All of these are boxes. If there are no limits, why do you need creativity?'

This is Stretchonomics through and through – without limits, there is no need for creativity. We cannot ignore our limits, but we can work around and within them. So we must define our own box then think creatively inside it. It was Albert Einstein himself who said, 'If I had one hour to save the world, I would spend fifty-five minutes defining the problem and only five minutes finding the solution.' Defining your box will help you stop from straying into that place beyond the Stretch Zone, where ambition and commitment aren't aligned, whatever your challenge.

The Power of Learning

Remember Carole Dweck and her principles of fixed and growth mind-sets? We've already seen how thinking 'inside the box' encourages creative problem solving. We often hear from the people we work with that they are 'not the creative type' or 'are rubbish at creativity'. Is success, therefore, out of their reach?

There was a time, not so very long ago, where the very apex of the art of creativity was... brainstorming. Brainstorming, we were told, allowed the mind to roam free. There was no shame in brainstorming. You could pluck the wildest, most fanciful ideas out of the air and, even if they were totally unrealistic, it didn't matter; it got the creative juices flowing and, if we brainstormed enough, we'd be sure to hit upon an answer. Yet there's a problem with brainstorming and, increasingly, creatives across the world are coming around to this way of thinking. The problem? It doesn't actually work – not to mention it being intimidating for those who don't feel comfortable showing off in front of their peers or are doubtful of their own capabilities.

Sure, it can be fun to throw crazy ideas into the mix – but craziness isn't real creativity, and it doesn't drive success in the real world. As the late, great David Ogilvy once said, 'if it doesn't sell, it isn't creative.' There's a reason that advertising creatives work so hard on the brief before they get going, and that they work in small teams, or that most entrepreneurs don't decide on their business ideas by inviting over twenty friends for a 6 hour working session fuelled by fizzy drinks and donuts. Classic big company brainstorming doesn't work because it often ignores the importance of the brief, it doesn't give people enough time and it values quantity over quality. 'No such thing as a bad idea', 'You have to have lots of ideas to have a good one'. Bullshit!

The Creative Problem Solving Process has been a part of the curriculum at a New York university for almost seventy years.[17.] Founded by academic Sidney Parnes and advertising executive Alex Faickney Osborn, the process depends on a very simple edict, one with which you're now familiar: valuable creative ideas occur within constraints, not without them. Parnes and Osborn begin by showing their students how to state their problem clearly – or, in Stretchonomics terms, how to define their S, T, and R, their 'box'. They then advocate breaking the problem down into smaller chunks, before generating ideas to deal with each sub-problem. You might think that a structured approach like the CPSP is in direct opposition to how the mind of a freewheeling creative works, but by giving creativity borders we are challenged to think differently – and the very best professional creatives we've worked with operate in this exact way.

The journalist and author Jeffrey Baumgartner summed it up like this: 'Highly creative people tend to follow this process in their heads, without thinking about it. Less naturally creative people simply have to learn to use this very simple process.' What Baumgartner is getting at is that creativity is not an innate talent bestowed upon a special few by an accident of biology. Creativity isn't magic. Like everything else, it is a skill we can acquire by dint of hard work and effort. It's a classic example of the power of Carol Dweck's growth mind-set. If we choose to believe we can change and learn, our potential becomes so much greater.

How Ideas Grow: Action, Reaction, and Action Again

We have worked with big corporates for more than twenty years and we have noticed a fundamental issue with their approach to developing new ideas to launch to market. They all tend to use a process called 'stage gate'. This was initially designed by NASA to project-manage space programme initiatives and is now applied to everything from credit cards to new flavours of crisps. The principle is that an original idea is created and goes through multiple steps in its development: periods of work (stages) and periods of review, when investment decisions are made as to whether to progress or not (gates). There can be between three and eight stages and gates before a product or service gets formally launched to the world.

As with any process, the challenge comes not from its core principles or even design (which in this case are extremely sound and sensible), but in its application. The challenge with this sort of process is that, when poorly applied, it can add time and complexity not reduce it, as was the original intention. It can create a sense that getting the idea to market is the main job in hand. It can create a focus on the idea and not execution. As Ogilvy suggests, the real challenge is making money from it, growing the business. Success is not completing the process but in the outcomes reached when the new product is finally released to market. In recent years, many companies have turned to entrepreneurs – who are often, out of necessity, faster and more resource efficient – for inspiration. The rise of 'lean start-up' thinking has been hugely influential in the last five years, well beyond the world of start-ups. It's a clear cut, three stage process and it works like this:

1. Begin with an untested hypothesis. This might be a product or a service whose viability for market you're seeking to test out.
2. Don't hang around. Get out there as quickly as you're able and engage in communication with your customer base. Use their

feedback to directly influence your SCOPE and TARGET. Look to learn and then…

3. Adapt. Follow your learning with agile development. Synthesise the feedback you're receiving back into product development. Speed up the process of turning your ideas into reality.

This process has the advantage of being much more action orientated and focused on what is happening in the market and not in the process. Stage gate has become a symbol, in many companies, of having a fixed mind-set (the inability to be wrong), as innovation teams push ideas through the processor at all costs. Meanwhile, lean start-up is a symbol of having a growth mind-set, in which we are almost looking to be wrong in order to improve and progress.

'Pop Ups' (a temporary retail space) have changed the way we think about retail. The main advantage of a Pop Up to an entrepreneur, apart from it being a cost-effective way to access retail space, is that it gives new businesses a chance to get out there quickly, meet their customers and get direct feedback on what they're doing. In short, Pop Ups are a fast way of finding out what works and what doesn't, an *in vivo* experiment which avoids the temptation to overthink an idea in the way big corporates do. It allows entrepreneurs to try new things which can improve performance. We have tried it ourselves with a booze brand we created and funded a few years back. There is nothing like learning in the real world, rather than in a world of Powerpoint and Excel.

We saw a brilliant example of the vulnerabilities of big company processes (and the idea over execution mentality) a few years back when we were working with one of the world's largest confectionery companies to improve their performance at the all important festive period. We happened to be in their office in July when the first batch of their new chocolate Father Christmas figures arrived. This was an exciting moment in the company's calendar and we sat around a conference table in an anonymous office in an equally anonymous business park, all eager to unwrap our chocolates, the first of hundreds of thousands to come off the production line. The characterization of Father Christmas on the foil wrapping was perfect. His red and white suit took us back to memories of our childhood; his warm smile and open, jolly face was the very picture of Christmas. But as we peeled back our wrappers, there was some nervous murmuring around the table.

It wasn't hard to see why. While he was still wrapped up, the jolly Santa in our hands was the very definition of festive fun. But now that he was undressed, things appeared a little less family friendly. The chocolate had been moulded into a shape which would perfectly match the design of the foil: the outline of a traditional bobble hat, a smooth face running down to a gently sloping gut, shapeless legs and two large hob-nailed boots poking out of the bottom at a 'ten to two' position.

All around the boardroom we all were getting dutifully stuck into six inches of festive chocolate phallus, all the while trying to balance personal dignity and ambition, suppressing school yard giggles and trying to cope with a growing sense of crisis. Table manners barely came into it. Sometimes real-world testing matters, before you hit the big red button.

The key to the growth and success of any idea is exactly this: having a feedback loop that provides information you can react to in order to improve your idea. If you are launching a space rocket NASA-style you need 'stage gates' to make sure nothing goes wrong – but if you are launching an app, a whisky brand or new retail idea or running a marathon, then real-world feedback is invaluable.

We've seen the way ideas grow through action and reaction up close and personal. It is a perpetual criticism of consultants that, while we might talk a good game, we never put our own money on the line. We have always strived to tackle this challenge head on – not only by aiming to be as accountable as possible in our work with clients, but also by creating our own new businesses to ensure that the talking-to-walking ratio doesn't get too out of kilter.

A few years ago, we combined forces with another partner to create our own booze brand, Albion Racing Club. We deliberately created Albion the 'wrong' way round. Most people, especially in the booze industry, make a product before they brand it – but we had long held the belief that, in some quarters, the seriousness of the 'craft' and the process was confusing, and that this made some categories in spirits – especially whisky – quite inaccessible. Therefore, we created our brand first – and only then decided what liquid to put in the bottle. We subsequently bought up and branded vintage vehicles, commissioned art for posters, invested in 'shot-ski's' (those who know, *know*!), did a deal with promoters in the Alps, and made a film with some amazing young film makers… and all before we had distilled the batch at scale.

We learnt a huge amount from our Albion Racing Club experience – most of which has made us better at our day jobs, and much of which inspired the thinking behind this book. Granted, some things we learned were less helpful, like how to bobsleigh with horrendous hangovers, make decent cocktails from the contents of a hotel mini bar, and run product tastings under a garden gazebo in a storm. It was through Albion that many amazing people came into our lives; some were interested in the product, but more came to us because of the metaphorical "Club" we had created. Albion was how we first met Laura Penhaul and the Coxless Crew, among many other exceptional men and women – from Tiger Moth pilots, to injured servicemen, from adventurers to professional sportspeople, from drinks' enthusiasts, Land Rover nuts and a whole community of makers and entrepreneurs. And it stretched us in lots of other ways too. Having established the brand, we were very quickly stretching ourselves in ways we hadn't thought possible – meeting and trying to win over some of the top bartenders and mixologists in London, or running hours and hours of tasting sessions in the 'grocer to the Queen', Fortnum & Mason's in London. These tastings were a critical part of our learning loop – we gained so much knowledge from hearing how consumers described the taste of our drink and how they reacted to the branding – and it reinforced, for us, the value of receiving feedback in real-time, synthesising that feedback into your product, and taking new and improved versions back to market.

The Pivoting Principle

It wasn't always plain sailing with Albion Racing Club. We made our share of mistakes and hindsight is a wonderful thing. Albion has not (yet) been a huge financial success, and who knows, it may never be, but as a learning exercise it was, and continues to be, invaluable. Perhaps the most fascinating thing that the business revealed was that, soon after our launch, it became clear that people were interested in the brand and not just the booze. Using the brand as a focus, we went on to sell British-made Albion branded bikes through a partnership with Quella, as well as clothing and adventures. We didn't set out to use the brand in this way, but when the opportunities came up, we leapt on them.

In tech companies this kind of change of direction is relatively common. So much so, in fact, that it even has a name: the pivot. One of the most legendary pivots in the history of tech is the transformation of Odeo into Twitter. Odeo began as a network where people could find and subscribe to podcasts. But, when iTunes began to take over the podcast niche, Odeo's directors decided that a drastic change was needed. In order to decide what that change was going to be, the company gave staff two weeks to come up with the best ideas they could. At the end of that time, Jack Dorsey and Biz Stone had come up with a status-updating micro-blogging platform. Twitter was born.

The omnipresent dating app Tinder was also created by something of a pivot. The team behind Tinder once worked for

Hatch Labs, a small part of a company called IAC which owns, among other businesses, Match.com. Hatch Labs was dedicated to coming up with new ideas (hence the name!) and the technology behind Tinder was originally intended to be used for a location-based customer loyalty app. At some stage the pivot happened (the close proximity of Match.com might well have helped) and the location-based dating app was created.

As we've seen, the willingness to pivot, to flex and change according to feedback from real world performance, is crucial. EXECUTION isn't rigid and can be tinkered with, perhaps even transformed along the way. The willingness to adapt, to want to learn, and to keep stretching has to be at the very heart of everything we do. It takes confidence to pivot. If your ego is fragile and mind-set fixed, it can be tough to admit you are wrong; you might well end up going too far down the wrong road. If you can recognise that there are other, better paths, you are more likely to be successful.

In our experience, some big companies can be like January gym goers: they create a plan, stick to it rigidly for a short period of time, lose interest and wander off and do something else. But successful entrepreneurs often don't have 'something else' to wander off to. They have one company, one business, one workforce and so will innovate and pivot until they find a profitable way forward. For them, making evolution and the willingness to pivot a part of their makeup is a vital component contributing to their eventual success. Ask yourself: are you sticking too rigidly to an execution that doesn't work? If our marathon runner isn't developing the stamina for his race by going through his training routine, is he right to stick doggedly at it... or is tinkering with the way he does things, switching up his training routine and investigating other things that might work, the right thing to do? The Scope and Target don't change, but the Execution can be flexed.

Stand Out Ideas

Marketing guru Seth Godin is prolific but one of his recent books stands out. It is called *Purple Cow*. Godin's call-to-arms is a simple but memorable one. Taking in the swamped marketplaces of the world, the copy-cat advertising methods, the deluge of similar products being foisted on consumers each year, Godin argues that the only way to actually make a success is to innovate an idea that instantly stands out from the crowd – the way, say, a purple cow might be the first to be spotted in a herd of grazing Aberdeen Angus. For Godin, being 'very good' isn't enough. Very good is… bland. Only the remarkable matters. Being brave counts.

Creating Purple Cows is all well and good but, as we see it, there are two challenges a 'purple cow' has to confront. Firstly, sooner or later, everyone else's cow will be purple too. As soon as people realise that being purple makes you stand out, they bathe themselves in purple paint, and, pretty soon, you're not standing out at all. A quick scan of the music industry shows you that the artists whose careers have lasted longest are constantly evolving their sounds. Would David Bowie have lasted as long as a relevant musical force if he'd remained Ziggy Stardust forever? Would Madonna still be with us if she'd remained the Madonna of *Borderline, Holiday,* or *Vogue*? Artists like this have all managed to stay ahead by… consistently changing the colours of their 'cows'.

Secondly, although the desire to be remarkable is strong, there's another desire that often sits within us – and that's the desire to fit in. The behavioural economists among us call this 'social proof', and it works like this: when a person is in a situation where they're uncertain of the right way to behave, they often start mirroring the people around them. Unconsciously, we all do this. We all want to fit in. It's what makes groups of people start to share the same mannerisms and behaviours. Just think how similarly people who work together often dress! And brands and businesses can be subjected to its influence as well. Being remarkable – being a purple cow – often means acting against the general trends around us, going against the crowd – think about Brewdog and their 'punk' attitude. The fear of standing out for the wrong reasons is often stronger in us than the desire to rise up above our contemporaries. Consider it another form of loss aversion: by nature, we'd rather protect ourselves from losing reputation than take a risk to gain it. This stops individuals and businesses from stretching, innovating, and trying to be remarkable.

The simple fact is, whether we're individuals, companies, famous or not, it's difficult to be remarkable. Think of the world of elite sport, where the rules are codified and the opportunities for reinvention are rare. We can't all revolutionise our events in the way Dick Fosbury did when he pioneered a new way of doing the high jump in 1968.

And the same is true for the world of business. It isn't easy to be remarkable – there is, after all (with apologies to *Spinal Tap* fans), a fine line between genius and idiocy. What's more, we've already seen that, to be successful, we don't necessarily need an idea that will disrupt and reinvent the world. The quest to find a Purple Cow can lead us astray. Stand-out ideas are powerful when executed well, but when we're so intensely focused on our purple cows, sometimes we overlook the myriad of other advantages we can get by tweaking the things we do, one increment at a time.

Think of these as our 'marginal gains' – the one per cent improvements which, when added together, make a significant difference. A famous exponent of this principle is Sir Dave Brailsford, the general manager of the cycling collective Team Sky, and the man responsible, as performance director of British Cycling, for a period of spectacular success for the United Kingdom. Sir Dave's policy was simple. Rather than make big sweeping changes to his teams, he focused on a breadth of tiny details. Everything was looked at in intimate detail – whether that was having cyclists take their own beds on the Tour de France, dusting tyres to get extra grip in the Velodrome, or experimenting with different aerodynamic suits – you name it, he looked at it and made countless tiny adjustments on the road and track alike. The results were as spectacular as they have subsequently become controversial.

Sir Clive Woodward, head coach of the England rugby team which won the World Cup in 2003, had a similar approach. He claims that he set out to do one hundred things one per cent better, and again, the results were spectacular. So too did Andy Flower, England cricket's head coach from April 2009 to January 2014. Flower had embraced the teachings of Billy Beane and the Oakland As baseball team, as related in Michael Lewis's book *Moneyball*. Beane and his colleagues had embraced statistical detail, seeking to give their baseball team – then an underfunded and unfashionable franchise – an edge, and eventually turning them into championship winners. Like Brailsford and Woodward, Flower was a man who lived and breathed for the 'one per cent' – the imperceptible changing of a batsman's grip, the type of shirts they wore, what food was eaten and when – that could, put together, give a team a considerable advantage.

In the world of business, you need look no further than international delivery service FedEx to get a good sense of the power of marginal gains. In 2007, after much theorising and brain work, FedEx implemented a 'no left turn' policy as part of a sustainability drive, meaning that, from that moment on, all of their delivery routes in the USA were changed to avoid left turns. This might seem an almost imperceptible change, but cumulatively it had an enormous impact. In the first year this was put into practise, it shaved nearly 30 million miles off FedEx's delivery routes, saving 3 million gallons of gas, and reducing CO_2 emissions by 32,000 metric tons – the equivalent of removing 5,300 passenger cars from the road for an entire year, and drastically reduced the number of costly accidents. It is a phenomenal example of both thinking inside the box and the power of marginal gains.

A person or business invested in marginal gains is constantly looking to stretch themselves and learn. They're constantly looking at the day-to-day things they can do better. They're not content to sit and coast. To live in the world of marginal gains is to know that your EXECUTION is a constantly evolving thing. Marginal gains matter and they're all around us, everywhere we look. Unlocking these is something we will explore in Techniques.

In sum

So what have we learned about EXECUTION which might help us in the Stretch journey?

1. Ideas are the easy bit. Originality (and persistence) in execution is the difference between success and failure.
2. Thinking outside the box is a flawed concept. Define your box using S-T-R, get inside it, and start being creative...
3. Creativity isn't innate. It's a muscle that can be honed, and it takes hard work (and brainstorming is mainly nonsense).
4. The only way to make an idea better is to go out there, try it, and learn (think of the Naked Father Christmas).
5. Sometimes we need to be brave enough to stand out in how we execute. If it isn't working, it's OK. Some things don't work. Don't give up. Pivot – or learn!

CHAPTER 5: **TECHNIQUE**

- Spotting and bridging the skills gap
- Why our brains are not like busy nightclubs!
- Managing the big 3: 'skill fade', 'automaticity' and the importance of 'psychological safety'

Picture our marathon runner. Over the last weeks he's perfected his training runs and is breezing half marathons; but he is struggling to get faster. His mile by mile times won't budge. Nobody said this stretch was going to be easy, but he begins to wonder: what if I'm not right for this? What if a marathon isn't the event for me?

We've all reached that point in an endeavour when, faced with challenges that seem insurmountable, we begin to question whether this is the right thing for us, whether we're perhaps *suited* to some other endeavour instead. Perhaps our marathon runner really isn't cut out for the full twenty-six miles. Perhaps he just doesn't have the 'talent' – perhaps he's not a runner. There could be a tendency to be overwhelmed by the challenge and react by wondering if we might be naturally incapable of achieving the things we've asked of ourselves.

You might have heard about the 'talent myth'. Writers like Matthew Syed have unpicked the idea of natural talent (especially in sport) and shown it for what it is – a trick our minds play on us, that pounds us down and keeps us from growing.[18.] For Syed, success is not driven by talent alone; what we think of as 'talent' is actually just another word for a developed competency, and we develop those competencies not because of a trick of our genetics (though sometimes this helps), but via good old-fashioned practise and good technique. The more we do it, the more 'talented' we become. To Syed and other writers like him, it isn't talent that sets apart the very best from the rest of us.[19.] It's technique combined what fellow sociologist Angela Duckworth calls 'Grit' – the passion and perseverance that drives certain people among us to achieve great things. Malcolm Gladwell talks about the principle of 10,000 hours to achieve mastery in something. He and Syed both point out that it's the time spent honing the right skills, doing the right things, that matters. For our runner it might be a question of heel strike, of stride length, of breathing and practicing these technical aspects of his sport. In running, as in anything, Technique can be learned. It can be improved. There is room for stretch. Yet, while experience is important – having the persistence to stick with it will increase your chances of success – running for 10k hours will not make you an elite marathon runner. It's time to talk about... TECHNIQUE.

Context Is King

It isn't easy to accept that the things that have made us successful in the past won't necessarily make us successful in the future. Somehow this seems to undermine our pride in the things we've already accomplished. In 2010, Team Sky set themselves the goal of winning the Tour de France within five years. This was a big bold Target at the time and, to achieve it, they realised that they would first have to put in place the right people, skills, training methods, sports science and race tactics to have a chance of succeeding. They soon highlighted their star athlete, Bradley Wiggins, as being their best hope – but Wiggins was neither mentally ready, nor in the right shape, to win. Team Sky had been successful until now but, if they wanted to achieve the even greater levels of success exemplified by winning the Tour, something was going to have to change.

In Stretchonomics terms, this meant a complete transformation of Team Sky's techniques. And Team Sky soon identified Australian sports scientist Tim Kerrison as the man to bring about that transformation. Kerrison's background was in swimming and rowing – and this meant that, by importing techniques from another sport, he was able to help Wiggins reinvent his entire approach. Kerrison transformed his training methods, moved the training base to Tenerife so that more high altitude training could be achieved, and even boosted Wiggins' upper body strength.

Team Sky had been forensic, and at the heart of their crusade was the fact that their approach was specifically designed for Wiggins, and specifically for the 2012 Tour. The following year, the course would be different – so each year presented a different challenge and, accordingly, a different kind of technique. A Tour winner, Team Sky had calculated, needs to get close to a threshold power output of 6.7 watts per kilogram of body weight. In 2011, Wiggins was at 6.57. Therefore, he was tasked with losing weight, as well as boosting his power output by doing more long climbs. The approach would have been different from the approach they took for fellow cyclist Chris Froome the following year.

Let's break it down further. In simple terms, what Team Sky had done was to develop an understanding of exactly what was required to win, taken stock of their current situation, and then – by hiring Kerrison and developing various new Techniques – sought to bridge the gap between the two.

One of the challenges of being a consultant is that you don't necessarily pick the sector in which you become expert. We could spend hours chatting lubrication of wind turbines or industrial cutting fluids, high performance skincare or women's lingerie, the Russian retail landscape or the latest developments in consumer credit and tech, crop science or even blockchain and Bitcoin. One area we have ended up knowing more than most about is booze, and in particular beer. In case you are getting bored of the boozy references, we have taken the view that it is a bit more accessible and interesting than some of the more technical niches in which we work... Apologies if this is not the case! Anyway, we were working with a client in East Africa. Much of East Africa is rural and poor but, like lots of the developing world, it is changing fast and cities like Nairobi are growing daily. In these urban areas, well over half of all alcohol is 'informal alcohol' – low cost, illicit brews proliferate here. They're often dangerous to drink and are a serious public health challenge.

Our client, a beer company of international repute, was keen to see if they could give low income drinkers a safer alternative to home brews. However, they were a premium branded company, and their knowledge of the techniques needed to operate in this end of the market was limited. The Scope and Target were no doubt stretching – they would have to make a product they had not made before and get it to places and consumers they didn't know much about, probably working with partners they didn't know – and all with no guarantee of success.

They identified their Scope – to make and distribute low cost, safe, decent quality beer. They set an ambitious Target (this was not going to be a dabble, they were chasing a big number). They had the Resources, but they soon identified that they had a 'skills or capability gap'. They were not currently making or selling drinks into this part of the market, but they did have one thing on their side: they recognised their failing and sought to address it.

Think back to Team Sky and their accomplishment with the 2012 Tour de France. When embarking upon a new stretch, there's a simple process we can all go through to define where we are and what we need to do. Firstly, we need to understand what's needed to achieve our Stretch ambition. Our beer company knew they had to learn about their new consumer base, what they wanted and what price point they would find affordable (about half the cheapest current products available). Then they had to develop cheaper ways to brew and package their products, as well as new ways of marketing and distributing the drinks to areas and people with whom they had little contact. The things which made them successful in the past elsewhere would not help them in this challenge. Once we understand the things we need to achieve, the next step is to assess what your current skills and capabilities are. By comparing the two, you've identified your 'skills and capabilities' gap. Then, finally, having highlighted the most important gaps, the areas where you'll need to improve, we can go out and either develop, acquire or create the right new techniques to succeed.

Team Sky had been through this very same process as they prepared for the 2012 Tour: first, they had identified what they needed to do to achieve their stretch ambition; then, by appraising where they were at, they had defined what their 'skills gap' was; and, finally – by hiring sports scientist Kerrison – they had acquired the new techniques to help them succeed.

Developing new Techniques was exactly what our beer firm did as well. In order to reduce the costs of production and meet an affordable price point, they developed kegs with manual pumps instead of the usual costly glass bottles, and beer that tasted good even when not ice cold – things they had never done before. New marketing techniques were developed to replace their traditional billboard and in bar advertising upon which the industry tended to rely. To do this, the company's managers created a series of 'roadshows' in Nairobi's informal settlements to help people understand what the beer was (how it was made, how it tasted etc). The key to unlocking came when they partnered with a local bank. Lacking the infrastructure or systems, they worked with the bank which would provide micro-finance (small short term loans) to individual vendors to allow them to buy stock, which they would then sell on to bars and friends. This devolved supply chain is now used by many companies to tackle 'the final mile' in the developing world. Anyone who has been to Lagos will have seen the blue-and-white 'Fan' ice cream vendors on their bicycles or in Johannesburg, the 'Danimamas' selling dairy products in the informal settlements, who are financed in exactly this same way. The real driver of success was a series of new Techniques applied in combination to unlock a previously impossible, unviable market.

When it comes to developing the skills, processes and tools to deliver your Stretch ambition, there is no 'one size fits all' solution. Everyone's situation is different. But the process our client went through to achieve their goals can be applied to anyone, anywhere – and what it boils down to is knowing the *context* of your stretch. Your own individual context is key, and it's set, just like the 'boxes' in which we're all stretching, by your SCOPE and TARGET. Without knowing our SCOPE and TARGET, we'll never be able to identify the appropriate TECHNIQUES to take us to where we're planning to go.

The success we can derive from using our S and T to understand our context cannot be understated. But nor should the dangers of not recognising if and where there's a considerable skills or capability gap (which is often the case when stretching). Plunging into any endeavour without properly understanding what's needed to achieve a goal can lead to unforeseen and unhelpful coping strategies further down the line. This might be what's happening to our marathon runner when he hits his brick wall and finds he can run no further. Before he embarked on his training, did he go through these three simple steps? Did he properly understand what was required of him from a time, fitness and stamina perspective? Did he embark on a loose training plan, without properly interrogating how big his skills gap was and what he might need to do to fill it?

Time and again we've seen teams and individuals in big companies grappling for coping strategies, when asked to reach a stretch goal without knowing or looking to see if there's a capabilities gap or if new Techniques could help. The result is teams feeling out of their depth, demotivated, and suffering from the personal reputation damage that can come with 'failed' projects. What's clear is that – whether it's drinks in Africa, or our marathon runner toiling his way along his course – only a proper assessment and understanding of where your company is truly at will allow you to identify the appropriate new Techniques you need to fulfil your ambition.

New Techniques Are Out There – Make Them Yours!

In our experience, one of the biggest challenges companies face when trying to deliver a Stretch ambition is believing that their ordinary ways of working can be applied to their new, more ambitious goal – that what got us here will be the things which will help us in the Stretch Zone. We worked for a global agro-chemical business who produced and marketed products for farmers. Part of their business was tasked with entering the consumer market, targeting home and allotment gardeners. While the opportunity the company had identified was the right one – there was a gap in the market – they soon came unstuck; they had not appreciated how different this task was to their normal way of working. They didn't have the basic marketing and 'consumer insight' (understanding why we buy what we buy) skills to make this work, and nor did they understand the consumer route to market (having to work, as they would, with different partners from the 'traditional' farmer focused retailers and distributors). In fact, all they really did understand was how to make a superior product... and kill weeds better than anyone else. This is all well and good – but what use is a superior product if you don't know how to sell it or can't persuade people to buy it, or even get it to them? For this company, identifying the skills gap and then closing it was vital – so we introduced them to new tools and techniques designed to win in consumer markets. They then hired new marketers and sales executives with experience of working with gardening retailers. Only be reinventing their TECHNIQUES did they have any chance of delivering their growth ambition.

There is one simple rule when it comes to reinventing your TECHINQUES: look outward, not inward. When we look inward, all we can do is replicate or iterate upon the things we have done in the past. Perhaps we'll make incremental changes – but incremental changes, taken alone, are rarely enough to get the job done. Only by looking at what others are doing, and thinking laterally about what new techniques and tools are out there, can we hope to find the changes that are right for us.

In our experience, if there's one thing that big business needs to do to start looking outward, it's to be more open and flexible. For many businesses, this is a thorny issue. After all, most successful businesses are successful *because* of their inflexibility. Or, to put it another way, they've found a system that works for them and that's already reaping dividends – so why risk changing it? For a certain sort of company, inflexibility counts. We were once faced with the challenge of helping a highly successful and efficient baked beans manufacturer to create a range of new products, and our assignment came with one simple caveat: not to mess with the existing system. They were making a million cans of beans a week. We could do anything which didn't mess with 'the system'. There was a disconnect between the ambition and what they were willing to commit. They wanted to grow but didn't want to change. This is a common type of conflict. Perhaps you've hit the point where your core business is running smoothly, but where you've reached a plateau or bottleneck, one you're struggling to push through? Perhaps you've exhausted your capacity to grow by relying on the same old methods and need to extend beyond it? Well, the only way of doing this is by looking to different skills and approaches, ones you might not have internally. And the only way of doing that is to look out.

The world of elite sport is particularly good at looking outward and finding advantages from other fields which it can bring into its own. Think of Eddie Jones, the England rugby coach who has reportedly taken to using drones during training. Or think of Sir Clive Woodward who, in preparation for the 2013 Rugby World Cup, famously employed the services of vision coach Dr Sherylle Calder to improve his players' judgement of precisely where the ball is, as well as the line, length and angle on which it is travelling.

Jones has also taken inspiration from Spanish physiologist Alberto Mendez-Villanueva and imported a methodology called 'tactical periodisation' from the world of soccer. Tactical periodisation is a training method that focuses on four specific movements of a game and how one transitions to the next. It's designed to fine-tune the decision making process and help players respond quickly on the field, by training them at an even higher intensity than the game itself. 'Every day,' says Jones, 'we train a specific parameter of the game. We have one day where we have a physical session and do more contacts than we would do in a game. Then we have a fast day where we try to train for at least 60% of the session above game speed. We don't do any extra fitness. It's all done within those training sessions. Because of that we've improved our fitness enormously.' Importing the technique from the world of soccer helped Jones to extend the number of consecutive wins the England rugby team were capable of securing.

Bringing outside experts in also revolutionised the workings of Italian football club AC Milan. Their 'Milan Lab' was established in 2002 after a costly new player suffered a career-threatening injury and, consequently, never fulfilled his potential. In response, the club brought in Jean-Pierre Meersseman, a Belgian chiropractor who believed that, with careful thought, the club could either prevent or predict costly injuries and also enhance a player's career beyond their expected age of decline. 'Age doesn't exist,' Meersseman said. 'What counts is that you are physically and psychologically ready to play. It doesn't matter if you are 21 or 41.' Meersseman's team set about collecting vast quantities of data on squad members, incorporating techniques from kinesiology, psychology and neurology along the way. Their work paid immediate dividends. In the project's first full campaign, the club reported that the total number of practise days lost to injury dropped by 43%, and the use of medicines went down as much as 70%. Player injuries had dropped by two thirds and, as a consequence, the team saw success on the pitch as well, winning both the Champions League and the Coppa Italia.

And all this because the club was willing to look out there and bring back expertise that, until then, had no 'natural' place in football.

We have witnessed the same in our partnership with Harlequins Rugby Club. For a few years now, GPS trackers have been placed in players' shirts in both rugby and football (in training at least). Elite teams use this technology to try to increase performance, driving 'marginal gains', reducing player burnout and minimising injuries. But in the real world the data created by 'in shirt technology' does not always give the backroom staff what they need. Even more importantly than making sure nobody was hiding in a bush to miss the team run, one of the main uses of this technology was to reduce the injuries of key players. The problem, though, was that, in rugby, most injuries come from the impact of two or more individuals banging into each other and not from running a long way or quickly. 'Shirt tech' doesn't measure this accurately – at least, not yet – so the analyst teams ended up counting and rating impact instead of relying solely on GPS data. They started with an untested hypothesis (that how hard you train impacts injury), got out there and tested it, then learned from the results and modified what they were doing. The salutary lesson here was that, even when there is new technology, new techniques need testing and exploring. Harlequins, like many others in their situation, look to other sports to learn and find inspiration.

The world of business can learn much from the world of sport about looking outwards, cannibalising others' techniques, and bringing them back home. For instance, in the business world there can be an obsession with 'doing' at the expense of planning and preparation, but any successful sports franchise will tell you that, in their own world, planning and preparation is all. The vast majority of an elite athlete's life is spent training, with only a fraction of a career spent doing the job itself (some estimates suggest just 20%). No company could ever hope to duplicate this, but the emphasis on understanding what makes someone good at what they do can give added advantage in all kinds of different business scenarios.

Sport is only one of a hundred other fields we might look to when exploring techniques we might bring back to our own worlds. In our experience, big business has much to learn from the military – not only, as you might expect, in the fields of leadership and strategy, but in more specific areas of capability too (and no, we are not advocating turning the car park into a parade ground for early morning marching). One particular field the military has always excelled in is logistics – and the international freight organisation FedEx has made it its mission to import this wisdom into their own operations. FedEx have regular discussions with military organisations about what they can learn – it's a two way street, with the military also seeking to leverage FedEx's operational techniques as well – and it has already reaped great rewards for the company. FedEx's logistics, their supply chain and their policy of 'command control' – in which managers are delegated greater responsibility for making decisions, rather than being micro-managed from above – are all directly inspired by lessons acquired from the armed forces.

Of course, looking outward does not have to mean looking as far away from home as the world of elite sports, or the theatres of a military conflict. Even the most adept and experienced businessperson does not have the experience of his neighbouring firm, and it might be that there are techniques we can borrow or import from other businesses around us. Think of that most unlikely of business unions: the marriage of convenience made between Apple and Nike in 2006. Both giants in their own fields, Apple and Nike had independently set their sights on what they thought of as a fascinating new direction the market might take: wearable tech. Nike didn't know enough about wearable tech to take this journey alone, and Apple didn't know enough about personal fitness or athletes – but, together, their resources were greater than the sum of their parts.

Nor does it have to be a bigger, more outwardly successful company that we look to when thinking about new techniques. In fact, the trend is often in the opposite direction. Big companies are powerful but they can be cumbersome, ungainly things. They have so many moving parts, their methods and techniques become so entrenched, focused on efficiency which makes them inflexible, that it is difficult for them to pivot, be nimble or change direction fast. Think of them as a juggernaut, or a stampeding elephant: powerful but difficult to steer. These companies are not impervious to the shifting markets in which they operate and, as we've already seen, to remain unchanging for too long is to get left behind. Sometimes they *need* to adapt and, when they do, they often look to adopt the tools and techniques of much smaller companies.

In our EXECUTION chapter, we've already looked at the methodology of the Lean Start Up method, how its principal aim is to get a start-up's products into a consumer's hands much faster. The tools and methodologies it promotes might not come naturally to businesses who already have a significant history or market presence, but they're increasingly being adopted by these firms as a way of staying ahead.

Think of the US corporation GE. At 125 years old, GE could not be further from our natural definition of a start-up firm, but that didn't stop the industrial giant from adopting certain lean start-up techniques to succeed. In 2012, GE incorporated FastWorks, a branded internal approach to translate lean start-up principles and other disruptive strategies across all its core businesses. GE recognised the need to combine the speed and agility of a start-up with the scale and resources of a large enterprise – and they're not the only ones. The research and advisory firm Gartner estimates that, by 2021, more than half of the world's established corporations will be leveraging lean start-up techniques to increase the pace and success of their growth and transformation, while many are already exploring and testing via venture teams or labs.

Think of your TECHNIQUE as a constantly shifting thing. Like the other stars in our Stretchonomics firmament, our techniques must change and adapt if they're to stay alive. Don't stand still. Don't rely on your own quick wits and imagination to come up with all the answers. Why would you? The answers are already out there – often being refined and tested by people with much more time and experience than you.

The Power of Habits

Closing a skills gaps inevitably means developing new talents… so let's explore what happens when we learn a new skill. It won't come as any surprise that new skills require overt attention in order to execute them. That's what your brain is doing whenever you set about doing something new – throwing raw resources at the problem in hand. According to Nathan Spreng, neuroscientist at Cornell University, the first step in learning a new skill requires a huge amount of focus. Spreng uses the example of learning to swing a bat in baseball. Focusing on both bat and incoming ball, trying to connect one with the other (and all while synthesising all the advice you've been given about the 'perfect swing') – all of this takes an intensity of concentration we are not used to in our day-to-day lives. And yet... the more you practise, Spreng says, the less you have to think about what you're doing. You might have used the phrase 'second nature' yourself. Second nature is when something that once demanded intense focus feels as if you knew how to do it all along. One of our godchildren was explaining, ahead of his grade one piano exam, that he wasn't really concentrating on his fingers. 'They just sort of know what they're doing,' he said. It's why a baseball player swings his bat without consciously reckoning when and where the bat might meet the ball. And it's the difference between having learned a new skill... and having fully incorporated it into who we are.

When learning to swing a golf club, scans of brain activity show multiple areas of the brain being engaged in order to complete the new task (albeit often with mixed results). The fact is that, when we learn a new skill – whether it's learning the guitar, providing customer support over the phone, playing chess, or doing a cartwheel – we're changing how our brain is wired on a fundamental level. Science has shown that the brain is incredibly plastic – that it doesn't actually 'harden' at the age of 25 and stay solid for the rest of our lives, as many of us have a tendency to believe. While certain things, especially language, are more easily learned by children than adults, we have plenty of evidence that even older adults can see real transformations in their neuro-circuitry. As we practise – whether by writing every week, hitting jump shots on the basketball court, or playing *Call of Duty* – what we're actually doing is triggering patterns of electrical signals through the neurons in our brains. Over time, the pathways that these electrical signals are blazing become harder and more pronounced – effectively increasing the speed and strength of the signal. It's like going from dial-up to broadband. Practise makes the connections more powerful with every iteration – until, eventually, the things we had to concentrate to do don't require nearly the same focus at all. Recent studies even suggest that we should 'over train' – in other words, that we should keep on practising even after we believe we've cracked a new skill, further strengthening the new connections in our brains.

But why? And how does this influence the decisions we're taking in Stretchonomics? Well, accomplishing our Stretch ambitions requires us to close the skills gaps we've identified. Closing those skills gaps requires adopting new techniques. And if those techniques aren't fully inculcated into us and our organisations – if the neural pathways we've blazed are weak – then we can't rely on the techniques we've adopted.

The goal, when acquiring any new technique, has to be one of 'automaticity' – for the skill to become so natural to you that you perform it almost as if on autopilot, leaving the rest of your brain with the processing power to deal with other tasks simultaneously. For a surgeon this might be the awareness of everything else happening in the operating theatre, and the mental space to properly acknowledge if things are going wrong. In big business, it might be managing your stakeholders, or 'fighting fires' elsewhere in the organisation. Whatever our new skills are, it's only with regular use that they become automatic to us. Without regular use, the neural pathways we've marked out become weaker. Imagine them rutted with potholes, overgrown by weeds – returning to nature, like any abandoned road. Something of them will often remain – if you played piano as a child and then don't return to it until much later, you will often find your fingers 'remembering' notes and chords, even though your waking mind does not – but the connection will be weaker.

In the military they recognise this and call it out. 'Skill fade' matters. When it's life and death, automaticity is key. It's crucial for us to be aware of this kind of decay or deterioration. Reinforcing a new habit has to be a constant process; taking a new skill for granted is, in fact, just letting it go. What is so interesting is how those of us who are not in the worlds of the elite military or sports often allow our basic skills to fade as we acquire new ones. We don't value the skills we have. We feel the basics should be left behind as we get more experienced. We often seek, cherish and celebrate the new. We seem to operate a 'one in one out' policy – but our brains are not a busy nightclub. They have they have capacity to stretch and grow.

The value of automaticity and actively preventing skill fade couldn't be greater in the world of Stretchonomics. Once we've identified a skills gap, we need to:

1. Identify the new skill you (or your team) need to acquire to fill that gap.
2. Identify the Technique you need to fill the gap (and remember to think broadly – be open)
3. Practise – and over-practise – the Technique, until it becomes a habit.
4. Keep performing the Technique on a regular basis, to defy the natural degradation of 'skill fade'.
5. Granted, this list was a hell of a lot easier to write than it is to put into practice but the principles are clear.

Environmental Factors

No doubt about it, humans are complicated creatures. And as challenging as it can be to acquire a new skill and then make it a fundamental part of how we operate, it's harder still to break an old habit. Those neural pathways in the mind might be subject to gradual skill fade, but dismantling the ones we've already built – for instance, when a fast bowler needs to make an adjustment to his action in cricket, a rugby player develops new sprinting techniques, or when a guitarist has picked up poor habits that have now become second nature – is always going to be a challenge. But it's a challenge we have to face if we're truly going to reach our Stretch ambitions.

Neuroscientists from John Hopkins University, in Baltimore, have demonstrated that, when people see something associated with a past reward, their brain flushes with dopamine. We've come across dopamine before – it's that addictive chemical released by your brain to reward you whenever you've done something of which it approves. Well, the neuroscientists at John Hopkins demonstrated that our brains flush with dopamine – with a sense of *reward* – whenever we see something associated with a past reward, not only when we accomplish something. They've shown that our past experiences bias the way we act now by flushing our brains with chemicals designed to reward us.

And we can harness this simple science in our attempts to embed new techniques. We already know that we need to encourage practise and repetition to transform those newly-acquired techniques into lasting habits – and encouraging this through reward and recognition becomes vitally important. In a sports team it might be the analysis which follows a big game, the break down and comparison of stats or the carefully edited video packaged sent to key players to help them improve. In a business environment, it might mean setting specific, measurable goals with each employee or the entire team. Positive reinforcement can shape both behaviour and enhance an employee's self-image – and both of these things put us in the best possible place to start breaking old habits and replacing them with new.

Whatever your organisation is, making sure it's an environment that welcomes change is vital to reaching your Stretch goal. Peter Senge's 1990 book, *The Fifth Discipline*, popularised the idea of the 'learning organisation', going on to sell more than a million copies worldwide. The Harvard Business Review listed it as one of the seminal management books of the past 75 years – and it isn't difficult to see why. According to Senge, while all people have the capacity to learn, the structures in which they function are often not conducive enough to reflection and engagement to ensure that learning happens.

In our experience of the corporate world, it's very hard to find a true learning organisation. Many corporations have concrete learning processes and practises in place, but not many of them have a truly supportive learning environment. In business it is all too easy to pay lip service when results are looking good – and, when they are bad, the desire to foster a learning environment tends to disappear as business leaders search for other, more tangible answers or reasons for decline. The tendency for companies to rely on the old ways of working – to sink back into the sanctuary of the Comfort Zone – can be over-powering. Rather than breaking out and trying new things, people are often encouraged to revert to old tried-and-tested methods... and asked to work harder. This reductive thinking rarely leads to transformative success. Google have identified that supporting this via creating a culture of 'psychological safety' is key. Giving employees time and support to learn is a key competitive advantage. Instead, when you are looking to introduce new techniques in the quest to reach a Stretch goal, ask yourself if you have these three simple building blocks in place – and, if not, what changed can you make to your organisation to make certain they are?

1. Does your environment support learning? Do members feel 'psychologically safe' to make changes? Is there an appreciation of differences, an openness to new ideas, and have you built time for reflection into your busy schedules?

2. What learning practises and processes do you have in place? How is information generated and shared, to the betterment of everyone? What training programmes do you have? How open are you to experimentation with process?

3. Does your own leadership, and the leadership of others around you, reinforce learning? Leaders who signal the importance of

spending time on identifying problems, sharing knowledge and reflecting on lessons learnt can inspire an organisation. What kind of leader are you?

According to a recent study, organisations with a strong learning culture are 92% more likely to develop novel products and processes, 52% more productive, 56% more likely to be first to market, and 17% more profitable than their peers.[20.] The data is clear: it might be easier to become a learning organisation when you're a small start-up (often out of necessity), but even companies with a long track record of doing things a certain way can and do transform themselves. The first step is to acknowledge that change is needed.

One Technique To Rule Them All

Is the way I have always done things right? Can I change? *How* do I change, and is my environment one that welcomes changing and challenging new Techniques? All of these are questions you'll have to confront when defining what techniques are important for your particular stretch.

Let's recap:

1. Try to spot the skills gap – the difference between what's needed to succeed and the place you are now – and do it early!
2. Look beyond your immediate environment. Who else is facing the same sort of challenges out there? Who can you learn from? Find them and learn from them.
3. New skills need to be practiced and over-trained in order to become automatic.
4. New skills and habits aren't automatically ours for life. They atrophy if we don't use and reinforce them. We need to fight 'skills fade'.
5. Our brains do not operate a 'one in one out' policy – we all have room to grow and add new techniques

6. When we belong to a learning organisation, it makes it so much easier to incorporate new tools, techniques and ways of working into our daily lives… but it needs support and actively managing.

CHAPTER 6: **COURAGE**

- Types of courage and the power of 'Little c'
- The (positive) power of failure
- Risk, fear and the chemistry of courage

Training for a marathon isn't easy. At this point we feel we can disclose that we have both run them in the past, with mixed success and levels of enjoyment and discomfort. When a runner sets out to achieve the goal, they are often filled with enthusiasm. But, after too many early starts, too many long, boring runs through grey drizzle and sleet, they can begin to wonder: *is it worth it*?

The call of the Comfort Zone is strong, particularly at 6am, when it's pissing down outside and the temptation is to put the run off until tomorrow, to have just another hour in bed. Stretchonomics is about facing up to these moments, having a word with yourself, and pulling your running gear on (be it metaphorically or literally).

There's a reason why many of us struggle to step out of the Comfort Zone. In fact, there are two major and basic human traits that work against us. The first is that we are designed to seek out comfortable habits. Our cave-dwelling ancestors were grateful for what comforts they could find. Their lives were packed with dangers – so, if ever there was a brief respite from the privations of nature, or the threat of becoming some other creature's prey, they would take it. To our hunter gatherer ancestors, the idea of the Comfort Zone would have meant an abundance of food, and a dry, safe cave in which to rest their heads (probably – our expertise does not extend into pre-Cro Magnon evolution). And you know what? Biologically, we are still the same species that lived in tribes and hunted woolly mammoth. We're still programmed the same way, to seek out the Comfort Zone and wrap ourselves in it whenever we can. We're not programmed to enjoy and embrace Stretch. In fact, we're programmed for the opposite. It's said that, by the time we reach the age of 35, we'll have tried 80% of the new things we'll experience in our entire lives (and as we're both over 35, this one statistic has been more motivating than pretty much anything else in driving us on to our own stretch challenges, both personal and professional – from creating a booze brand, writing this book, to making moonshine in the kitchen, learning the inner workings of vintage tractors to long distance downhill ski racing). There is a caveman or cavewomen in us all – looking for safety and certainty. Life in the Stretch Zone means actively challenging this, sometimes on a daily basis. It sounds unpleasant but it can be intensely rewarding.

We inherited something else from our caveman ancestors as well: the compelling desire to fit in with others. Mark Earls, the author of *Herd: How To Change Mass Behaviour By Harnessing Our True Nature*, sums this up perfectly when he says, 'We are a super social animal… a herd animal.' Being programmed to get along can be a good thing. It is, after all, one of the many advantages human beings have over other animals, and one of the things that eventually led to mankind becoming the dominant power on this planet. No other apex predators can live in such close proximity and in such vast numbers – imagine the carnage of millions of lions living in a few square miles of each other. The challenge is that stretching ourselves can mean standing out. It means embracing our individuality, pushing ourselves, transforming the way we do things by degrees. To stretch is to actively choose *not* to be part of the herd (or as Tough Mudders would have it – being part of a smaller but different herd), to get out of the warmth and comfort of our cave. To put it bluntly: stretching goes against our hard-wired biology.

A step into Stretch requires tackling these natural instincts with... COURAGE.

What is Courage?

There is a huge amount written about courage – some good and some bad. It is an area where simplicity helps cut through the noise. We have a favourite definition:

Courage is not the absence of fear, but the ability to face it.

Like any good quote, attributing it to a particular source is complex. For this one, Nelson Mandela is in the mix, but so are Mark Twain, 'Biggie' Smalls, Winston Churchill and even Bruce Lee. The list would be an inspiring mix for a dinner party or could make for an interesting celebrity 5 a side football team (with Churchill in goal!). But these things are all about context – so we are giving it to England Rugby World Cup winner Will Greenwood, the man who first brought it to our attention. A few years ago, we had accompanied Will – among others – on the freezing ascent of Mount Kilimanjaro in Tanzania. There on the mountainside, only minutes before the final trudge to the summit with the temperature twenty degrees below zero, Will gathered everyone in a tent and delivered a speech that has been with us ever since. *Courage,* he said, *is not the absence of fear, but the ability to face it.*

The great thing about the thought is that it is practical. So, when we stepped out into the swirling dark, more than a little intimidated, we could immediately put it to use. Here, almost 20,000 feet above sea level, on the slopes of a dormant volcano, we were all very much out of our Comfort Zones, and had been for several days. But thanks to Will, our little team were able to tell themselves that it was OK, perhaps, to be afraid.

Let's be frank: of all the things written about courage, there is – in our experience – very little worth listening to. In writing this chapter, we tried to define exactly what courage is, and this sent us off on a wild goose chase into some of the more bizarre hinterlands of the self-help market. But when it comes to Stretchonomics, we need a rigorous definition of what COURAGE means to us – and, at 3am on the slopes of Kilimanjaro, we had found it. To us, it means not refuting our fears; it means accepting that actions have consequences – but that these should not make us step back from the course we've chosen to take. That is courage – facing our fear and using it to help us on our way.

What Will Greenwood said to us on that African mountainside, with the wind roaring around us and the snow strafing across our vision, isn't just apt for those with an adventurous spirit. It's good advice for us all – in business, as well as in life. No matter what stage we're at in trying to achieve our stretch goals, we need COURAGE as our constant companion. We need COURAGE to make us take that first step. We need COURAGE so that, when we're faced with a problematic situation (as we will be – problematic situations are the very things the Stretch Zone is made of) we don't back down. COURAGE helps us confront those moments where our emotions impact our performance – as they inevitably do – and turn them to our advantage. It was the Harvard psychologist Stephen Pinker who said, 'The refusal to acknowledge human nature is like the Victorian's embarrassment about sex, only worse: it distorts our science and scholarship, our public discourse and our day to day lives.' For us, COURAGE is the ability to make a decision and to stick with it, even when it feels a bit scary. Accepting our fears, our inhibitions, our emotions more generally, and working to reduce their negative impact – that is true courage, Stretchonomics-style, and in this chapter we're going to explore exactly what this means.

The Twin Types of Courage

We have worked with corporations large and small, with tiny start-ups, performance specialists, sportspeople, soldiers and academics – and, through them, we've seen that courage can take many different forms. The company board taking the bold gambit to start expanding overseas. The soldier recovering from serious injury to a start a new life. The rugby player who backs themselves to beat the last defender instead of passing to score in the dying seconds. All are examples of courage, but they are different. Courage is nuanced. It depends on context. Like stretch itself, what's courageous for one individual or firm might not be courageous for another.

In Stretchonomics we try and think about two distinct types of courage. We call these 'Big C Courage' and 'Little C Courage', and here's how they work.

Big C Courage is about big, bold gestures and commitments that don't come around too often. The spectacular game-changers, the headline grabbing investments, the leaders who declare 'Follow me, men, I'm going in!', the risky play in the dying seconds, the moments when you might put your house on the line or leave a perfectly good job to start your own business. These enormous moments, when a life might pivot on a single decision, are important, but in Stretchonomics we think of them as the outliers. They rarely come around but, when they do, they shake the very foundations of what we're doing – the all or nothing gamble, double or quits. They are often seen as heroic, especially if they pay off, and are the most visible manifestations of courage.

Little C Courage, meanwhile, whilst easier to overlook, is just as critical (if not more) to any endeavour. It is less glamorous, it does not get the headlines or the medals – but without Little C Courage, any Stretch can unwind. Little C Courage consists of the innumerable small, daily gestures that are about doing the right thing, fronting up to potential conflict, not taking the easy way out, and not taking a backward step in pursuit of your targets. These are the often unseen decisions of choosing the right thing over the easy thing. Little C is dealing with our twin caveman traits of being a bit uncomfortable and not necessarily fitting in with everyone else.

For a successful Stretch, it's important that we acknowledge and understand both types of courage. We need to be ready for Big C Courage when the opportunity comes around, but along the way we need frequent doses of Little C courage. Big C gestures are the catalysts to great change or great achievements, but without the baby steps of Little C Courage there is a danger that they are empty gestures or un-kept promises. Little C Courage will advance us, inch by inch, every day.

We faced both Little and Big C Courage challenges with our booze brand Albion Racing Club. Big C Courage was needed to make the break and set it up in the first place, writing cheques without knowing for sure if there would be any return on them, starting a business for which we had limited hands-on experience, challenging the usual ways of creating and building an alcohol brand. But Little C Courage was there too. We needed to tackle all the things we did for the first time, whether it was sorting out the legal elements of the trademark, running tasting sessions (what on earth does one do in a tasting session? What are you supposed to talk about?), setting up our social media, selling directly to bars from a suitcase (an actual, not a metaphorical, one), or signing up partners in joint ventures agreements. Each needed Little C courage to give it a go. The joy of a small company is that, if you don't do it, it doesn't get done. Procrastination and turning a blind eye don't work. Little C means facing up to the tricky little things you would rather avoid.

Think about the twin tracks of courage. To make a success of a new venture, we need both Big C courage to take that first declarative step, and Little C courage to get through the many smaller challenges we'll face along the way. That's as true for an entrepreneur as it is for our amateur runner, who needs both the courage to sign up to the race and get out of bed on a wet winter's morning.

Vitamin C

Big C gestures have a huge impact on the success of any venture, big or small. Perhaps the first Big C gesture you'll make when undertaking a Stretch is a demonstration of commitment – whether that's a leadership team in a business committing to a new course of action, or an individual telling others about achieving a personal goal. Whatever your Stretch, without a Big C commitment, success is going to be almost impossible to achieve. Paul Leinwand and Cesare Mainardi put this beautifully in their book *Strategy That Works: How Winning Companies Close the Strategy-to-Execution Gap*: 'When you don't commit,' they say, 'you risk becoming scattered among a variety of objectives… You gain a right to play in many markets, but a right to win in none. You risk becoming a company that perennially promises great things but never seems able to deliver.' And who would want to be that company? Who would want to be that person? How often do we end up as the busy fools, trying to do too many things, without having the courage to stop, focus and make a real play for the things that matter? We recently worked with a client who cancelled all his meetings for six weeks while he faced a particularly gnarly challenge. He needed his team to have the thinking time to tackle the challenge – to deal with the important, not the urgent. Undertaking the challenge itself required Big C courage, while cancelling meetings and other commitments for so long required a daily healthy dose of Little C.

Stretch can require a certain amount of courage. In our experience, it's often the bigger companies who lack this collective courage. It might seem paradoxical, but the big businesses who can afford to take risks often don't, while those who are just starting out, or don't have the necessary financial resources, are much less risk averse, again often drive by necessity. When a person is hungry for something, they will often be more courageous in order to achieve it – and, in Stretchonomics, this means being more willing to take those Big C steps. But when a person is comfortable and secure – when they feel they have a lot to lose and not much to win – their instinct is often to play it safer. The same goes for big companies. Big companies are social animals too and the need to conform can have an effect on them as well. Remember the Thaler experiment and how we fear losing something twice as much as we love the idea of winning the same amount? Big companies are as susceptible to this as individuals. Just think about the typical large company approach to remuneration – a good salary and a small bonus, often related to overall group or company performance. There is not much to win and lots to lose (reputation, status – even the job itself).

In the land of big corporates, there is an amazing statistic. According to a study by Nielsen, the top 25 largest food and beverage companies in the USA in 2015 generated only 3% of total growth in that year in their sector, despite accounting for more than 45% of sales. In other words, despite maintaining an enormous piece of the pie, these manufacturers can only take credit for $1 billion of the $35 billion in sales from new growth. Isn't that stunning? The companies in this top list are mind-bogglingly large, with a combined turnover of nearly $700 billion dollars – about the same as Holland or Switzerland's GDP – with Nestle alone generating $90 billion dollars a year. Yet, with all this wealth, the best they can do is create 3% of the total sector's growth, while the small and mid-sized players account for everything else.

Liana Lubel of Nielsen explains this by suggesting that, 'instead of launching bold, category-disrupting innovations, they launch a lot of play-it-safe, *me too* innovations. They use consumer research as a way to prevent bad innovations from launching rather than as a way to explore ideas and make them better. This behaviour only succeeds at mitigating growth, which fuels the perception that innovation is risky.' Seen through a Stretchonomics prism, it's clear what's happening here: the stretch has stopped. Big companies reach a certain point and they find themselves slumping into a new kind of Comfort Zone, where they're unwilling to push themselves further. They might be talking Big C, but they're struggling with Little C courage, and the results seem to follow.

Not all companies are like this. Amazon is an extraordinary success story and shows no signs of slowing down. Amazon has a culture that is constantly innovating, looking for new things to try, and constantly testing their initiatives with their customers. In the way it conducts its business, constantly iterating new projects and designs, it shows Little C courage every day; and, in its bold gambits, isn't a stranger to Big C courage either. Some of these Big C commitments are unimaginably vast – just look at Amazon's purchase of Whole Foods in 2017 for almost $14 billion, a move which had the immediate impact of wiping millions off the share price of Whole Food's competitors on both sides of the Atlantic, including Walmart, Tesco and Sainsbury. Amazon is growing in every direction, and its success is built on courage. Scale doesn't have to preclude courage.

So too is the success of British athletics, or Team GB. The team's success at the 2016 Rio Summer Olympics, where it won 67 medals, was an improvement on the 65 it won in London in 2012. This was a remarkable achievement because countries invariably do much better when the games take place at home, and is made even more so when you look at the team's previous totals: 47 in Beijing in 2008, 30 in Athens in 2004 and 28 in Sydney in 2000. There is one Big C reason behind this success: total funding for UK sport ahead of Rio 2016 was £274 million, an increase from £264 million in 2012, which was itself up from £235 million in 2008, which in turn had risen from £71 million in 2004 having been £59 million in 2000. This is classic Big C – a bold gesture to make a vision come true. Ambition and commitment are aligned.

Or think of the British rugby club Wasps, who moved to a new home in Coventry in 2015 from their traditional home over 100 miles away, and immediately launched a retail bond with the aim of raising between £25 million and £35 million from fans and investors. Within days, the bond was oversubscribed. This bold, unprecedented move made the club one of the richest in its sport in Europe, allowed its debts to be paid off and, crucially, enabled the club to buy its own stadium. This was truly remarkable as, only three years previously, Wasps had been on the brink of bankruptcy. The future now looks rosy – thanks, again, to a Big C move.

Big C commitments are integral to the success of companies like Amazon, or sports teams like Team GB and Wasps, but they are nothing without the Little C being taken care of too. What would Amazon's purchase of Whole Foods look like without the Little C courage to make the acquisition work and carry on working in the long term? What good would Team GB's massive investment of resources matter if its athletes and coaches woke up every morning and, faced with another gruelling session, hit the snooze button and went back to bed instead? And so what if Wasps have raised enough money to wipe out their debts and re-establish themselves by launching an unprecedented retail bond? If they didn't back it up with the day-to-day grit and hard work a successful rugby club needs to survive, all it would be is a wasted opportunity. Amazon, Team GB and Wasps still had to do the work, day in, day out, in order to make these grand visions a reality.

Like these teams, it is important to commit to a vision, to put money where the collective mouth is and to back it up every day.

Learning Courage

Eleanor Roosevelt said, 'Do one thing every day that scares you.' American self-help guru Mary Anne Radmacher puts it very nicely. She writes that, 'Courage doesn't always roar. Sometimes courage is the quiet voice at the end of the day saying *I'll try again tomorrow*.' This is important as courage is not a genetically-predetermined characteristic. It's a skill, like creativity, like being a 'numbers person', that you can acquire with practice. It isn't the absence of fear, but the ability to choose to deal with uncomfortable situations. In lots of ways, Big C Courage comes easier than Little C. With Big C Courage, we can be in a distinct moment. We need enough courage to step into the unknown.. We might have reached a point where we need to change course and commit to a new direction. We might need to make one singular decision that will transform the lives of our loved ones or our employees. But with Big C we only have to cross the Rubicon once. With Little C Courage, we have to cross a multitude of smaller Rubicons every day – and this takes great reserves of stamina and resilience. With Little C, the adrenaline of one single moment cannot carry us through. Instead, we have to carry ourselves.

Think back to our TECHNIQUE chapter, and how we explored the power of habits. Habits, we saw, are what happens when a new technique acquires a quality of 'automaticity'. Well, what if the same principle could apply to courage? Maggie Warrell, the author of *Brave: 50 Everyday Acts of Courage To Thrive In Work, Love and Life*, describes courage as being like a muscle, and based on our personal observations we completely agree: the more we use it, the more courageous we become. We've already seen that the mind is elastic, with the power to rewire itself through rigorous mental training. Well, if the mind can do that, so too can the character.

We have an easy time accepting that the body can get stronger physically by practise and training. Yet many of us struggle with the idea that we could become more adventurous, become more resilient or more courageous. But courage can be a self-fulfilling prophecy. We might have to practise it, to fake it (to others and ourselves!), but eventually it becomes more 'normal' – and, without realising it, we've become genuinely courageous along the way. Like all of the best things, our courage is stretchy. We just have to be prepared to embrace the small moments when we can practise our stretch.

In fact, those small moments are all around us. Big C moments might be few and far between, but Little C moments are scattered throughout our days. If Big C is signing up for a marathon, Little C is every time you get out of bed to train when it's raining and cold. If Big C is jacking in the job to start your own company, Little C is phoning the bank to ask for money, or making your first sales call. Take a look at your life and you'll quickly see the opportunities are all around us. The world itself is your courage gymnasium.

Courage In The Face Of Failure

Courage and risk are hard linked. We need courage to take a risk. The bigger the risk, the bigger the 'C' required. The challenge is that we tend to see risk as what we could lose and not what we could gain. For anyone who has ever crossed the threshold of a casino there is the conflicting feeling that what could be about to happen is both good and bad. The fact is, there is an opportunity to both win and lose when we walk into a casino, but, if we're honest with ourselves, our human nature is drawn to the negative (think about Thaler). To most of us, risk means failure and the casinos know this – that's why they create games which could have massive pay-outs. As Caspar Berry would remind us, we're predetermined to fear loss more than we enjoy gain, and the natural response, on walking into a casino, is to be anxious that you'll walk out with much less than you walked in with. This risk is, of course, why gambling is such fun.

Why is it that so many of the technology 'unicorns' (the term for the rare beast that is a recently started company valued at over

$1 billion) are American, and specifically seem to hail from Silicon Valley? It's a question which has caused much hand-wringing in the European venture capital community. One theory is that, in Europe, investors have traditionally been very focused on the numbers, the business plan and the growth trajectory, while, in contrast, American funds have placed a greater focus on the people behind an idea and the talent making it happen (their expertise in 'Execution' and 'Techniques'). In Europe, so the logic goes, there seems to be a suspicion of 'failure', with investors wary of backing people who haven't hit the numbers in previous ventures. In the USA, meanwhile, they are interested in 'failure' – how many times you've failed? What did you learn? What would you do differently? The talent they're after have a growth mind-set, and in Europe we are more fixed with a more binary view of success and failure. As an aside, it's interesting how open most entrepreneurs are about things they have tried and got wrong (even in front of would be investors), and yet how often it is totally unacceptable to have the same conversation in large companies. As Eric Schmidt of Google says, 'It helps to see failure as a road and not a wall.'

Google is a place where attitudes towards failure are different to most companies of a similar scale. Peter Norvig, their Director of Research, has described it like this: 'If you're a politician, admitting you're wrong is a weakness. But if you're an engineer, you essentially want to be wrong half the time. If you do experiments and you're always right, then you aren't getting enough information out of those experiments. You want your experiment to be like the flip of a coin: you have no idea if it is going to come up heads or tails. You want to not know what the results are going to be.'

What Norvig is saying, in other words, is that failure produces the knowledge which will eventually drive us to success. In fact, according to this view, there can never be any success without failure, and this is a particularly sobering thought. The only way to find out what works is to eliminate what doesn't. It isn't for nothing that Thomas Edison said that, in his quest to develop a viable light bulb, he had not failed but merely 'found 10,000 ways which didn't work'. If we are stretching – are we better off being a politician or a engineer?

Perhaps it isn't surprising that a positive attitude towards failure is a feature of success stories in many different fields, not just business and technology. If some of the brightest stars in the world of music thought of failure as a judgement on themselves and their talent, we would be without some of the world's most successful and acclaimed songs. When 19 year old Minneapolis wunderkind Prince earned a three album deal from Warner Bros, he and his management somehow convinced the label to let him produce his debut album himself. The resulting sessions were difficult and expensive, riddled with tensions with executive producer Tommy Vicari, and they left the musician not only a physical wreck, but also $100,000 in debt – a figure which might not have seemed much later in his career, but was stratospheric to the teenager just starting out. Nor was the album itself as musically innovative and pioneering as his later output would be. The album produced only one modest radio hit in *Soft and Wet*, but beyond that was largely overlooked. Elton John, David Bowie, Genesis and the Beatles all had similarly inauspicious starts, and yet went on to sell many millions of records worldwide. Star Wars, the movie that ushered in an era of summer blockbusters and completely changed the face of Hollywood, was written off after it did poorly in its first test screening, with one member of the audience calling it 'the worst film I have seen since *Godzilla and the Smog Monster*', while it took the publishers of *Game of Thrones* three separate publications before the book started to garner readers, and it was only fifteen years later that it really took off, thanks to the critically-acclaimed HBO adaptation. How less rich would our culture be if these early setbacks had been written off as complete failures? How less fun would the world of music be if Prince, like many others, hadn't treated this early experience as something to learn from and used it to propel him to bigger and better things?

It's only natural that, in their early stages, ideas, businesses, careers and personal projects – indeed, endeavours of any kind – will face setbacks. It's a vital part of the journey, and it has never been summed up more precisely than in a 2013 tweet from Marcus Romer, the British film and theatre director. Entitled 'The Creative Process', Romer's tweet breaks the creation of an idea down into six neat stages. These steps are something we refer to in every important project we have worked on. This book has been through most of the steps, spending some considerable time on numbers 2, 3 and 4. We have the steps up on our office walls – it is the one piece of 'inspiration' we revert to whether we're race training or working on a challenging new project. It goes a little something like this:

Step 1: This is awesome
Step 2: This is tricky
Step 3: This is shit
Step 4: *I* am shit
Step 5: This might be OK
Step 6: This is awesome

Who knows, the journey Romer is describing might feel familiar to you? Once the post Big C rush of step one fades, it takes Little C Courage to work it through. When we embark on a new endeavour we are often driven along by the excitement and passion of beginning something. Then we become unstuck. We begin to question the project in which we're immersed. Then we question ourselves. The marathon runner in his third month of training, losing motivation, failing to see progress and feeling the stresses and strains of training will undoubtedly question himself and the whole idea of the race. It's these stages – 3 and 4 – that are the most difficult. It's here, when the going gets tough, that you'll need your Little C Courage the most: the courage to battle through the negativity and self-doubt, to carry on regardless. Perhaps you've made a negative judgement of yourself. Perhaps others have done it for you. Either one can impact your momentum. But if you want to succeed, you have to get through it. You have to grit your teeth and carry on.

These moments will undoubtedly come when you leave your Comfort Zone, but the good news is that there are things we can do to prepare ourselves for their coming. By accepting that you are on a journey, and that Stages 3 and 4 are just steps along the way, you can become resilient enough to ride through them. If you practise your acts of courage, build up enough muscle to persevere when the going gets tough, then you will get there.

The good news is that, inevitable as Stages 3 and 4 of Romer's process might be, there's light at the end of the tunnel. With a bit of careful thought and by applying some Little C Courage, Stages 5 and 6 – understanding and reconnecting with the things which made you excited in the first place – are right around the corner. Sometimes all you need is a little bit of inspiration and, for us, a quote from Winston Churchill. Among all of the other things he is famous for, Churchill's words on failure remain a source of solace: 'Success is not final, failure is not fatal; it is the courage to continue that counts.'

Taking all of this into account, you might be left thinking: well, what *does* it mean to fail? If these things are not failure, if failure is not the end of the road, then what exactly *is* it and how must we confront it? In Stretchonomics, to fail is an organic part of any process, and whenever you trip up or stumble, or fail to live up to your expectations of yourself in some other way, you might remember these four points:

1. **Few failures are fatal.** It is important to remember that, as economist and author Tim Harford writes in his book, *Adapt: Why Success Always Starts With Failure*, 'Few of our own failures are fatal... Success comes through rapidly fixing our mistakes rather than getting things right first time.' It is hard to put things right, and even harder to recognise and admit that something has gone wrong in the first place. As Mandela (or possibly rapper Tupac) said, 'I never lose. I either win or I learn', and if we can embrace this attitude, what were once 'failures' become learning opportunities instead.

2. **Failure Is Always Possible.** Keep in mind that few failures are fatal, but never lose sight of the fact that failure is a possibility. There is a danger of letting a supposedly brilliant plan lull you into a false sense of security. As the boxer Mike Tyson said, 'Everyone has a plan until they get punched in the face.' That punch could be coming at any moment. Don't waste your time devising a plan that you believe can outwit failure. Failure will outwit you every time – so just learn to be flexible and deal with it instead.

3. **Failures Are Stepping Stones.** Don't think of failures as the end of a journey. Imagine them, instead, as stepping stones along the way. Fear of failure is understandable – it's human nature – but it can be reduced if we start to look at each 'failure' as a means of progress, and not as a judgement on our talents, capabilities and character. If we think of each failure as a step forward, a move away from where we started and closer to our goal, then it becomes a very different thing. Be an engineer, not a politician.

The wisdom to accept that which you can't change and have the courage and patience to get through the tough times has a name. The poet John Keats described this strength in adversity as 'Negative Capability'. A strong sense of 'negative capability' makes a person happier because they don't let setbacks or the unknown get them down. This characteristic is also important for good leadership. You need the courage to either act – or, sometimes, not to act – when you're faced with uncertainty. You need to make decisions with confidence so that the people you lead are happy to follow you, even if what you're stepping into is risky. Indeed, it is interesting to note the number of very successful business leaders or sportspeople who have endured hardship in their early years, perhaps losing parents or siblings, as well as other adversities. These people, among others, have the ability to turn adversity into a strength. The author JK Rowling, the world's first billionaire author, famously said that she pinned her first rejection letter – of all the many she received – to her wall. It didn't depress her. It acted as an inspiration, for it was evidence that she was on her way, joining the journey many writers had gone on before her. And if that isn't an inspiration, then what is?

The Science of Fear

We've already seen how embracing our fears can drive us on towards our stretch goals. Fear, directed and put to good use, can be one of our greatest motivators. But there's another side to fear and courage that we can't overlook, not if we're to properly harness it in service of our Stretch. Because fear is not just a psychological response. Fear is physiological too.

When something happens to which we must react quickly, our adrenal glands flush our bodies with adrenaline. It's this hormone – sometimes called the 'fight or flight' hormone – which makes us more aware, more awake, more focused. We can all harness this adrenaline for good. But there's another hormone at work in our bodies too. Adrenaline comes and goes, but when we brood on a problem for a length of time, the body continuously releases cortisol. Exactly the right amount of cortisol helps a body maintain a good blood pressure, but too much cortisol not only affects the immune system; it *increases* blood pressure and blood sugar, and comes with a raft of other long term problems too.

What does this mean for Stretchonomics? Well, being in the Stretch Zone means tackling challenges regularly and, most of the time, that means fronting up to some level of fear. But if we're not prepared to deal with stress and fear in a healthy way – which means accepting it as part of a natural process – then we can end up living with the effects of cortisol flooding through our system full-time. This is bad for our personal health, and bad for our judgement too. Somehow, we have to be able to embrace our stresses, but not let them overwhelm us.

We need courage for this, but we need resilience too – and it's important to recognise that there's a difference between the two. It's this very difference that authors Khurshed Dehnugara and Claire Genkai Breeze discuss in their book, *The Challenger Spirit*. They argue that leaders of organisations facing a growth challenge need to be comfortable taking action and doing things that will be unpopular. This might cause them momentary stresses, but they need to develop an inner stability in the face of these circumstances, whilst still showing compassion for the feelings and anxieties of others. It's a tough environment to be in for a long period of time and requires what football manager Ian Dowie might call 'bouncebackability' – the capacity to get knocked down and keep coming back for more.

You might be tempted to think that resilience is about bearing the load, finding yourself in a tricky situation and *enduring* it. But putting yourself on a survival footing runs counter to every value of Stretchonomics. When we're surviving, that's all we're doing. Putting up with a situation, sticking it out just to get through – all of this saps your spirit. It might be a short-term necessity but long term it strips away all that's best about the Stretch Zone and strands you in one place, without any capacity to stretch or grow. When we're resilient, we're thriving. But when we're *enduring*, the opposite is true. You might even say that resilience is our adrenaline, the hormone designed to propel us through unscathed, while endurance is like cortisol – suppressing us, increasing the pressure we put on ourselves, and leading to chronic conditions.

Everyone experiences fear. Denying it is to deny our fundamental natures, and that's a conflict that will only lead to yet more damage further down the line. Instead, accept fear as part of your life. Accept that fear is normal, but also accept that fear can be fleeting. It doesn't have to be a permanent state of mind. Dealt with or channelled properly, fear will not last.

If you're afraid, you're not the only one. Abraham Lincoln worried constantly. Steve Jobs was paranoid, sometimes even delusional. Jackson Pollock suffered from intense anxiety. Too often we think of the most accomplished people as being fearless. This isn't true. The difference between Lincoln, Jobs, Pollock and the rest of us isn't a quality of fearlessness. It's a quality they acquired somewhere along the way that we can all acquire too, with just a little bit of practise: somewhere along the way, they learnt not to *fear* fear. 'Courage is not the absence of fear...' Here's what Josh Linkner, entrepreneur and author has to say about fear:

'Over the years, I taught myself to flip the fear. Instead of trying to eliminate fear (which can't be done), I use it to fuel progress. When facing a near-term obstacle that feels scary and overwhelming, I zoom way out and think about what I'm truly afraid of. I think about the regret I'll feel 20 years from now if I don't take the necessary risks to reach my full potential. I think about letting my family down, or not setting a good example for my kids. I connect with the disappointment I'd feel if I never rose to help my community or challenge myself to leave a positive impact. In other words, I force myself to focus on the long-term results of succumbing to my near-term fear.'

It doesn't get much simpler than this: instead of running way, we should connect with our biggest fears. Own them. Tame them. Use them to fuel our performances – not by railing against them, not by enduring them, but by embracing them as tools. Courage in the face of fear – this is where Stretches can be won or lost.

Continuing Courage

Courage is an important part of any stretch. Without courage, not only can we not start the journey – we can't deal with the challenges we'll inevitably meet along the way. Courage is critical because it drives the difference between what we *say* and what we really *do* (when no one is watching). So what have we covered here?

1. Whoever said it, we believe that 'Courage is not the absence of fear but the ability to face it'.
2. Stretch requires two types of courage – the heroic Big C and the determined, dogged and daily Little C.
3. It is impossible to stretch without having both – this might mean having to tolerate temporary discomfort in the service of the long-term goal.
4. Little C courage is like the Vitamin C you take everyday – and, if you do practise it everyday, it can soon become a habit, or gain the automaticity you need. Courage is like a muscle – the more you use it, the better you get at it.
5. A bit of fear can be a good thing – the brain chemistry actually drives performance.
6. Failure is not to be feared – it can be a very powerful step to progress (just don't make it a habit!).
7. Resilience is different to Endurance – there is a difference between hanging on and getting stuck in.

CHAPTER 7: **HUNGER**

- Staying hungry: the Two Chevron Principle
- The differences between internal and external motivation
- Staying in the Stretch Zone long term

It's the day of the marathon and our runner is up early. It's been a long road to get here, but he's made it. It took Big C Courage to launch himself into this Stretch challenge, and innumerable moments of Little C Courage along the way. But if COURAGE is taking the first step, our final Stretch element is about the desire to keep going, and, once you're done, to dust yourself off and get going again. HUNGER is the difference between our marathon runner tumbling over the finishing line and hanging up his running boots for good or signing up for the next race or another challenge. Hunger is to keep going through the Wall and to do it again, to set another challenge and to go again. To keep in the Stretch Zone.

On a recent trip we took to London's Design Museum, we were listening to a group of ten years olds asking very reasonable questions about the things they saw. What was a typewriter? A sort of computer without a brain, they decided. They questioned the bright yellow brick of the original Sony Walkman 'Sport'. They laughed at the bulky, colourful clam shell shape of an 'iMac', questioned why anyone would want a phone that was 'tied to the wall' and were intrigued, if slightly perplexed, by the concept of a fax machine. It made us realise just how much the world has changed in recent times (and how quickly the things we took for granted have now made their way into a museum). In the 21st century the pace of change is so acute that, over an average career of four or five decades, most of us will have to manage several careers at once, or at least change our work lives significantly a number of times. The current crop of CEOs out there would typically have grown up with black and white TVs. In a world where change is necessary and swift, we will have to be able to reinvent ourselves and, to do that, we will have to stay hungry and be willing to continually set ourselves new stretch challenges.

What is hunger and why do we need it?

In the world of Stretchonomics, we think of hunger as the desire and motivation to keep going, to keep pushing. Think of it this way: hunger is the difference between the likes of Madonna (the Queen of reinvention), U2 (the Kings of reinvention) or Blur and their musical rivals, Cyndi Lauper, Simple Minds, and Oasis. Perhaps we're doing these latter artists a disservice – and, indeed, more than one factor plays into the longevity of a musician's career – but the difference between transient success and careers that last decades and transcend the boundaries of genre is clear. Seen through a Stretchonomics lens, hunger is about not being *satisfied*. Think of Damon Albarn for a moment. Albarn began his music career in the 1990s with the Britpop band Blur. Having achieved extraordinary success, he was not content to hang up his musical boots. Instead, he went on to form the electronica group Gorillaz, then to make forays into World Music and movie soundtracks – and, to cap it all off, was awarded an OBE for his endeavours. Now compare that to Albarn's Britpop contemporaries in bands like the Bluetones, the Boo Radleys, Dodgy, Cast and even Oasis. Who displayed the most *hunger*? Who pushed what they had to the maximum?

There's a problem endemic to all forms of enterprise, whether that's music, business, sport or any other field of life. We set a goal, we apply our Little C Courage and keep persisting until we're successful... and then we take our foot off the gas. Every amateur road runner or cyclist, every triathlete or competitive swimmer, will recognise the feeling that comes after the big race or event. We call this the 'Ricky Hatton effect'. Ricky 'the Hitman' Hatton is the best British light-welterweight boxer of all time, successful at defending his WBU World Championship title a record 15 times, and also winning titles at two different weights. These achievements are remarkable, but scratch beneath the results and the story is even more interesting and complex.

Hatton is famous in the boxing world for his down-to-earth manner and approachability, in stark contrast to loud brash opponents such as Floyd 'Money' Mayweather, who Hatton fought a decade ago, narrowly losing in controversial circumstances. But Hatton was almost as legendary for his condition between bouts as he was for his guts and hard hitting inside the ring. He habitually gained huge amounts of weight after each fight. Sometimes, his weight would balloon by up to 30%. To put it another way: Hatton would gain almost a third of his body weight again while coming down from an event he'd been working towards for months. He made no secret of his love of pies and a pint – to be successful, he needed to recover in his own Comfort Zone before starting the process again, retraining his body until he reached his fighting weight again. That Hatton lived his entire career like this is testament not only to his love of a good pint, but to his mental power. Most of us struggle to get back and re-engage after a big challenge, but Hatton had the capacity to keep challenging himself, over and over and over again. He's a sporting version of Wayne Huizenga, or Laura Penhaul.

The Hunger Diet

Sir James Dyson is an inventor and industrial designer who went on to found the Dyson Company. At the time of writing, he is currently worth almost £8 billion. And do you know what else? He is famously no stranger to failure. He's failed time and time again, but it never diminishes his hunger to go back for more.

The invention that first made Dyson wealthy, his bagless vacuum cleaner, did not come into creation overnight. In fact, it took five years and 5,127 prototypes to perfect the design. And nor did his other inventions come easily. His 360 Eye Robot took seventeen years and more than a thousand prototypes, and the Supersonic Hair Dryer took four years and 600 prototypes. The numbers here are staggering. When you consider how many prototypes were made, how many years each one took and how much money these products are now generating, you not only end up with an object lesson in the power of failure, but an example of extraordinary hunger as well. After all, the income generated by just one of these inventions would be enough to establish a small fiefdom and ensure a person never had to work for the rest of their days. He had no 'need' to enter new markets or to create more products. Why, then, keep on and on – unless to satisfy the hunger that drives you?

If bagless vacuum cleaners aren't enough to inspire you, well, look to the story of Sylvester Stallone. Stallone was a penniless thirty-year-old with a dream when he wrote the screenplay for the first of his *Rocky* movies, the story of a down-and-out debt-collector who would go on to become a champion boxer. The script was quickly sought after by Hollywood, but the studios who were chasing it didn't want Stallone himself to star. Instead, they pictured Rocky as being one of the shining stars of the day: James Caan, or Ryan O'Neal, even Burt Reynolds. What's more, they were prepared to pay for it. One producer offered Stallone $30,000 – the equivalent of $1 million today – for the rights to the screenplay. It must have been a tempting offer, especially for a young man with only $106 in his bank account. But Stallone declined the offer. He was determined to make the movie on his own terms, and he was determined to star in it as well.

Consider it an act of Big C Courage if you will. But what comes next shows how HUNGER can characterise a life. *Rocky* eventually earned as much as $120 million in the United States alone, and spawned six further movies that have together grossed more than $2 billion worldwide. Not content with one transformative moment of success, Sylvester Stallone had the desire to go out there and do it, over and over and over again. And do you know what? He still isn't done. In 2013, he had to go back to basics, this time to convince theatre producers that *Rocky* could be a hit as a Broadway musical. The hunger paid off: Stallone managed to secure millions of dollars of capital investment, and the musical opened in 2014 to ecstatic reviews. In 2018, the second spin-off movie, *Creed II*, will be released to cinemas worldwide. Stallone's hunger for this series never lets up. It just keeps changing direction.

And this is the key to making the best of your HUNGER for your Stretchonomics life: establishing HUNGER in the first place is paramount, but going forward we have to find ways of maintaining it too. Sometimes pure passion isn't enough. So what techniques do we have to make sure we're more like Madonna… and less like Cyndi Lauper?

The Two Chevron Principle

In Stretchonomics, we think of the ability to keep going as the 'Two Chevron Principle'. Originally a French idea, but now popular in many countries around the world, these large arrows (chevrons) are painted on motorways, usually at forty metre intervals. The idea is that, if you keep two of these between you and the car in front, you'll have enough time to react if there's an emergency, based on braking distances.

Keep that image in mind, and now start thinking of it in Stretchonomics terms. We're not talking about driver safety here! Imagine, instead, that the car in front of you is your TARGET. If you get too close to it, it feels too easy and the challenge is gone –

and if you fall too far behind, the target will become disconnected, too difficult to reach. If, however, you remain *two chevrons apart*, you hold the tension. Your TARGET is tantalisingly out of reach but close enough to be motivating. You can easily picture what it would be like to achieve that target and the mere sight of it, two chevrons ahead, keeps you hungry, keeps you fighting every day to reach it. The Two Chevron Principle is about managing the distance between you and your goal, keeping the tension at exactly the right level to keep you fighting.

Carole Dweck would agree, and so would fellow sociologist Angela Duckworth. For Duckworth and Dweck, fulfilment comes not with success or failure, but with a tangible sense of progress. Did we finish the day in a stronger position than the day before, and do we have ambition to do the same the day after? For Duckworth and Dweck, this is where real happiness is located.

Seen through a Stretchonomics prism, this can only really be achieved if we find ways of maintaining our HUNGER. If we don't maintain our hunger, we can't maintain our progress and, at this point, everything stalls. Think back, for a moment, to Sir James Dyson and his £8bn fortune. We can't all be billionaires, but in our experience the same principles apply to us all. Dyson maintained his HUNGER by constantly shifting his TARGET, and the relationship between HUNGER and TARGET cannot be emphasised enough.

Dyson knew this. Once he'd completed his work on his bagless vacuum cleaner, he might have retired a wealthy man, but that kind of stasis would never have brought him fulfilment. Instead, he shifted his TARGET. He turned his expertise to other challenges: air purifiers, fans, hairdryers, and more (there is even now some talk of a Dyson electric car). He has most recently established himself as a champion for engineering in the UK, setting up and funding a Foundation and creating a number of innovation awards. And he's not the only one. Any follower of professional sport will know the peculiar mix of exhilaration and anxiety that comes with winning a major sporting trophy. In 2005, England cricket captain Michael Vaughan and coach Duncan Fletcher together steered their team to an Ashes victory that had not been seen in a whole generation. The euphoria was unparalleled. The team were honoured by the Queen and feted across London town. But when the return Ashes series came around in 2006-7, the team reached a nadir. They might have achieved a death-defying victory in 2005 but, a mere 18 months later, they were subject to a 5-0 whitewash that left Freddie Flintoff, one of the all-time great players, in tears on an Adelaide outfield. The unsympathetic Aussie press dubbed the tour 'Pomnishambles'. What had happened? Well, there were injuries, and poor captaincy decisions, and certainly a whole number of other factors contributed to the dispiriting outcome. But commentators were keen to point out one defining factor: somewhere in the transition from being underdogs to being champions, they'd lost their HUNGER. The thing they'd been dreaming about since playing school ground cricket had finally come to pass, and now the dream was diminished. Without the single motivating factor of that goal, they had nothing to reach for. They could no longer stretch.

In Stretch terms, we might say they stepped out of their Stretch Zone. After the excitement of the victory of 2005 had ebbed away, they were left rudderless, without a tangible TARGET of their own. It was only with a new coach and a new TARGET – to be ranked No. 1 in all forms of the game – that English cricket recaptured the mojo it had so fleetingly found. The lesson from both Dyson and the world of professional sport couldn't be clearer: to stay in the Stretch Zone we need to keep our HUNGER, and to keep our HUNGER alive we have to be willing to constantly shift our TARGET. It's no use reaching for the stars once we already have them in our hands. We have to reach further. We need to sign up to run again or get stuck into a new challenge.

Dyson showed it's possible, and across the course of writing this book we've met and spoken with a number of extraordinary individuals who are remarkable in their ability to keep going and stay inside the Stretch Zone. Will Greenwood, World Cup winner, TV commentator and all round good egg, now trains grass-roots rugby teams, as well as being a part-time maths teacher. Meanwhile, Laura Penhaul returned from her Pacific trip and soon after signed up to break another world record supporting Mark Beaumont in his challenge to cycle around the world faster than anyone before. She has supported elite tennis players on the world tour and, what's more, she's setting up a new business, and learning to pilot a lifeboat! But it isn't only exceptional people in exceptional circumstances that can keep their hunger alive. The right cocktail of HUNGER and TARGET can work for us all.

Motivate This!

'Many of man's greatest achievements are the products, or accidents, of ambition.' So says Neel Burton, psychiatrist and author of *Heaven and Hell: the Psychology of the Emotions*. According to Burton, the key is to pursue *healthy* ambition. 'People with a high degree of healthy ambition are those with the insight and strength to control the blind forces of ambition, shaping [it] so that it matches their interest and ideals. They harness it so that it fires them without also burning them or those around them.'

What Burton is getting at is one of our most basic human challenges, and one which plays an important part in the Stretch equation. What motivates us, as individuals and companies, to do what we do?

We all have a motivation. It's what we rely on to keep us going. But not all motivations are born equal. Some are external motivations – ones that come at us from the outside – and some are internal, ones which we have generated ourselves and cut to the core of how we view ourselves as individuals. Anyone who has failed to stick to a New Year's resolution to get fit may have struggled because their motivation was external rather than internal. If you made a resolution to get fit so that you looked better, or you were keeping up with friends, or doing it because that is what everyone does at that time of year, well, those are motivations driven by external factors – and, as such, you'll probably find it difficult to persevere when the going gets tough (as it invariably does). If, on the other hand, you want to get fit because you are driven by a burning desire to make yourself better for *you*, to tackle a specific challenge *for you*, if it's an ambition you have for yourself – and not just because you feel it's expected of you – you are much more likely to see it through. When it's your desire, you're only accountable to yourself, and the odds say you will make lasting change.

The war between internal and external motivations has been being waged for generations. You might have heard of the 'carrot and the stick' approach to motivating people – that people can be motivated to do something by either a reward, 'the carrot', or the fear of punishment, 'the stick'. But this traditional dichotomy gets it wrong, because both the carrot and the stick are externally motivating factors. They suggest that what motivates us is primarily worldly or material – that we're either seeking material reward or trying to avoid unpleasantness. In Stretchonomics we'd say that neither the carrot *or* the stick is ideal, because they're external motivators – they compel us to do things by some form of coercion, whether that's positive or negative. The only form of motivation that truly lasts is one that stems from our sense of self. And when we're setting our TARGET and developing our HUNGER muscles accordingly, we have to keep this in mind: are we setting a TARGET because of external factors, or because of internal factors? Who is more likely to succeed – the runner only contemplating a marathon to live up to an expectation his friends or family have of him, or the runner whose burning desire to complete a marathon comes from within himself? Is it driven by what one feels compelled to do or by something one yearns for?

These types of motivation also exist in the workplace. Externally motivated leaders in business are less effective; they're concerned with earning their bonus, pleasing their shareholders or avoiding damage to their own reputations. This can lead to safety-first, risk-averse behaviours or a symbolic approach to management where Big C projects are demanded and publicised. Externally motivated leaders value the short term over the long-term life of the organisation, and this can make an organisation vulnerable. Remember how Blockbuster video didn't properly predict the way the market was changing and was quickly bankrupted as streaming service Netflix came into the ascendancy? That's the perfect example of how an externally motivated organisation valued the short term over the long, was too risk-averse, and paid the ultimate price.

Conversely, internally motivated leaders are driven to make a difference, to leave a legacy, to make sure that the others around them fulfil their true potential. They chase the real challenges and tackle the fundamentals – and they're doing it for the satisfaction, not for the external 'glory'. These leaders inspire their employees and colleagues to match their internal fire, bringing out the best in everyone else. Employees become more critical in their thinking, more curious, more creative, and are motivated to become better at their jobs. They begin to enjoy their work more, to find fulfilment in it, and, eventually, happiness.

The difference between internally and externally motivated organisations became even clearer to us this year through work with one of our large corporate clients. In this business, every individual's annual performance was split between how well they had 'built the business' (sales) and how well they had 'built the organisation' (supported colleagues). Think of it as a kind of short-hand for how well an employee had looked after the short-term gains of the business – money through the tills – and how well they'd looked to the longer term, leaving the organisation in good health for a sustainable future. There is a forced balance between managing internal and external motivations together. It balances market share growth and share price rises, and the wellbeing of the wider organisation.

We have seen the difference between internal and external motivations first-hand. We played a small part in the setting up of the award-winning *One Minute to Midnight*, a research firm of which we are board members. As a research company, they examine the fundamental values we all hold and how these impact on the decisions we make, and in particular the brands we choose to buy (and how these vary around the world). As part of a huge global study, taking in 2,500 interviews across four continents, the team found that, although the values we hold as important vary across the world (for example, people in the UK value security and freedom of expression, while in China power and achievement are more highly valued), living in line with our values (whatever they may be) is the one thing that makes us all happy, wherever we live. Those who don't live by their true values were three times more likely to rate themselves as unhappy. We hold our value sets as being intrinsic to ourselves and, when we're obliged to live a life that doesn't line up with them, we feel disconnected and less fulfilled. Think of it like this: when we're externally motivated, we're being coerced – whether by punishment or reward – to behave in ways that don't accord with our own values. But when we're internally motivated, everything lines up – we have a purpose, a TARGET, that comes from the very fabric of who we are. And what could be more motivating than that?

In a company whose leaders are internally motivated, it's often the case that each person *feels* better. They feel personally invested in. They feel as if they have a say and a stake in what's going on.

They feel as if they themselves are acting according to their intrinsic values. Consequently, motivation levels are higher and business results often take care of themselves. An inspiring leader isn't necessarily one who, with an act of Big C courage, takes his or her employees 'over the top'; they could be a leader who listens, who is genuine, who values those around them. Over a coffee recently a client reflected on their recent work and their new boss: 'We felt inspired. If the leader of the business was motivated to become better, if they were looking to learn, to be prepared to make mistakes, then why wouldn't I feel the same?'

Creating Motivation

Being hungry matters, and there's clear evidence that people's internal motivations work more readily on them than external motivators. And one of the ways they do this, which proves so vital to Stretch, is by boosting our creativity.

If our motivations aren't internal – if they don't stem from ourselves, but are imposed on us from outside – can our hunger ever be genuine? Beth Hennessy, Professor of Psychology at Wellesley College, speaks eloquently about the importance of fostering internal motivation in schools. According to Hennessy, in her inspiring TEDx Talk, when we don't have internal motivation, creativity and curiosity are stifled. Hennessy identified several conditions which kill the power of internal motivation: when we come to *expect* rewards; when our time is restricted or controlled; and when we're constantly evaluated and watched. These principles are as true for our marathon runner as for any start up or corporate.

Hennessy's criticism of today's schooling system couldn't be more robust. She advocates paying closer attention to our children's internal passions and curiosity, giving them the time and space to solve problems, to work together, to try and fail. And the principles are exactly the same, whether we're in the classroom, the offices of a new start-up, or the boardroom of an enormous corporation.

The behavioural economists among us would call this 'motivation crowding theory'. Put simply: the presence of external motivators – like a big end-of-year bonus – crowd out internal motivators, like the pride we might take in a job well done. Emphasising external motivators actually acts to diminish internal ones, and all-round performance suffers as a result.

But keeping hunger healthy and alive isn't just a matter of finding the right motivation. 'Red Teaming' is an exercise undertaken in both the army and business as a way of *creating* hunger. A 'red team' is tasked with simulating an attack on the status quo or a new plan. The idea is that this simulated attack can expose vulnerabilities, create readiness for attack and suggest good responses, but it's not the details of the attack that interest us most in Stretchonomics. Rather, it's the way that the prospect of a Red team exercise influences the team about to be assaulted. The prospect of being tested often galvanises us to get the very best out of ourselves. It's a way of jump-starting our HUNGER.

Red Teaming is a critical part of the cyber-security world as well, with programmers routinely taking the role of hackers and trying to attack or destabilise their own systems. Think of it as 'hacking' by any other name: a group of expert coders are brought in to simulate a real attack on a cyber-security system, testing that system's response to an all-out assault. And the effect it has is just the same as in the military. It keeps the tension, it stops the original coders from resting on their laurels, makes sure they're at the top of their game by cultivating a sense of restlessness and expectation. It accepts that things move on and that an organisation or individual will be challenged. It's true that we all need to pause and rest sometimes, but we grind to a halt and eventually start atrophying if we get stuck in the Comfort Zone for too long. If we're not going forward, we need pulling back in, and being 'Red Teamed' can be a good kick in the pants (before a competitor does it to you for real). Red Teaming might feel like an external motivator – it's the threat hanging over us, propelling us on – but its effects are internal too; being aware of an external challenge can help us rekindle our internal motivation.

Whilst the power of internal motivation is clear, it's also important to recognise that external motivations aren't always unhelpful. There's little doubt, from our personal experience and observations, that we're at our most productive when the tasks we're undertaking are in line with our individual passions – but to ignore the power in external motivators is to ignore human nature (and Stephen Pinker has already warned us that this is a *very bad thing*).

If there's one group of people to speak to about the power of external motivation it's athletes. Most athletes would agree that the challenge of winning a championship, being awarded a medal, or breaking a world record, are external motivators that compel them to be the best they can be. In sport, it seems, it is natural to be driven by the external just as much as the internal.

It's this very idea that Costas I Karageorghis and Peter Terry explore in their book *Inside Sport Psychology*. According to Karageorghis and Terry, the way internal and external motivations work together produces the very best in a sportsman: the internal gives us the foundations for success, and the motivation to return day after day to training for the love of the process, but it's the external – such as the prospect of winning medals – that gives them the competitive drive to be the best they can be. Each athlete will have a different balance of motivations. We were chatting to an ex-Olympic skier, who had left elite sport for a career in business. A contemporary of the legendary Lindsey Vonn, she remarked in passing that, of her peers who had retired, half had not skied since finishing on the World Cup circuit. This struck us as utterly fascinating. She was saying that, for half of ex-racers, external motivation was the driver – the taking part, the competing, the winning. The other half had not lost their love of their sport and continued to ski for their own personal reasons, even if it might not always be at the utter limits.

The Sporting Life

Professional sport might be built around the external motivation of championships, medals and world records, but, according to the experts, it is an athlete's high level of internal motivation which compels them to keep going through the dips in form and confidence which are inevitable in a sporting career. For a comprehensive study, look no further than football manager Martin O'Neill. O'Neill was widely regarded as one of the most astute readers of players in the game and said that the best players to work with were always the ones who were unconcerned with how much money they earnt. Think of this in terms of intrinsic and external motivations. For O'Neill, the players who were primarily motivated by external forces – in this case, cold hard cash – were nowhere near as effective and easy to work with as those who were motivated internally, just by the love of the game. Rio Ferdinand, the great English defender, said he would have been a footballer even if he was on a minimum wage; Lionel Messi, who some people think is the best footballer of all time, says that the secret to his success is playing football as if he was still a child, with the same enthusiasm and motivation he had when no money or expectations were involved at all. You can see the same across other sporting arenas as well. Novak Djokovic, one of the most successful tennis players of all time, loves to train; he doesn't see it as a means to an end, but finds enjoyment and reward in the simple act of training itself.

There is surely some level of natural advantage in sport, but one thing is even more certain: these people would not have been able to make as much of their talents if they didn't have that inner drive, that internal motivation to carry on no matter what. Novak Djokovic has it right: internal motivation comes from loving what you're doing, not necessarily what you might achieve. According to a recent study by the Institute of Leadership & Management, the billions of pounds spent on bonuses has almost no impact on the commitment of most workers. In a survey of a thousand workers, a mere 13% said they are motivated by the prospect of a bonus, while a full 60% rated their enjoyment of their job as the thing that motivates us. Wherever we look in our work, we learn the same lesson. People might be hungry for external reward in the short term (who doesn't like a bit of recognition), but as a means to keeping our HUNGER alive into the future, we need to look a little bit deeper, into what drives us as individuals.

There is one more lesson regarding the magic of internal motivation that we can take from the world of elite sport, and that is the value of working in a team (remember – we are herd animals!). Let's admit, first off, that sometimes teams don't work; sometimes a team can be toxic and sometimes a team can be the difference between failure and success, and it all it depends on the combination of individuals involved. Yet Stanford psychologists Priyanka B. Carr and Gregory M. Walton have shown that even the subtle suggestion of being part of a team dramatically increases not only a person's motivation to accomplish certain tasks – but the enjoyment of them as well. To us, this is interesting. The value of working in a team is such that not only do team members work harder, they actively relish it as well. For if we are enjoying the tasks we have to undertake, what better motivator is there for a job well done? In this, we could all become like Novak Djokovic, not working solely because we have a goal in mind, but working for the joy of the process itself.

Carr and Walton's experiments showed that people in teams work harder and for longer, getting more involved and improving performance along the way. In one of their experiments, two groups of similarly skilled people were set the same puzzle which they would all work on individually. To one group, Carr and

Walton gave the subtle suggestion that they were actually part of a team by telling them that they were investigating how people worked together on this puzzle. To the other group, they gave no hints at all. The results that came in were clear: the group who thought they were part of a team worked for 48% longer than the other one. Walton was staggered. 'Simply feeling like you're part of a team working on a task makes people more motivated.'

Teamwork is not a new concept. It's the thing that elevated us from being lowly hominids, somewhere in the middle of the food chain, to being a species on the cusp of colonising the stars. Its power is imprinted on us so indelibly that, as Carr and Walton showed, its mere suggestion is enough to transform the way we think about ourselves and the tasks we've been assigned. In simple Stretchonomics terms: don't underestimate the power of teamwork for keeping your motivation and your HUNGER alive.

Hunger, the Open Mind and Measurement

There is one factor which links all of the thinking above, and that's the importance of being open and honest with ourselves. Whether we're in the world of elite sport, business, or anywhere else, being able to objectively appraise where we're at and where we're going is crucial.

Getting real time feedback, measuring and reviewing ourselves as we go – and doing so in as objective a manner as possible – is increasingly being accepted as the best way to drive both motivation (Hunger) and performance. For several years now, journals like the Harvard Business Review have been banging the drum for the end of 'the annual review.' Indeed, several companies – including Accenture, the behemoth consulting and IT firm – have recently done away with annual reviews altogether. Now, instead of annual appraisals, staff receive real-time feedback instead, allowing for continual improvement. Employees at GE now have a tracking tool – a PD@GE – which helps them and their managers keep track of their performance objectives even as they shift throughout the year. (GE is also changing the language of feedback to emphasize coaching and development rather than criticism.) GE employees get both quantitative and qualitative information about their performance, so they can readjust rapidly throughout the year. The technology does not replace conversations between managers and employees. Instead, it *drives* them, and, because the information is collected in real-time from the latest events, employees report that they find the information more credible. Meanwhile, managers too find the dialogues they have with their employees more meaningful because they're drawing on recent real-world evidence. Collecting and interrogating feedback in real-time rather than just once a year allows the managers of companies like GE to keep the chevrons moving at all times.

We've seen this principle being applied to elite sports teams – just think back to the GPS trackers in rugby shirts – but it's crossing over into our personal lives as well. Consider the increasingly all-pervasive fitness trackers many of us now have. These devices use psychology to motivate the couch potatoes and keen amateurs among us to start investing properly in our fitness. When you meet your daily goal, your Fitbit – or other fitness tracker – lets you know with a strong vibrating buzz. Not knowing exactly when that buzz is coming is like the variable reinforcement schedule that makes gambling so powerful.

Nike were an early player in this market. They were the ones who first pushed the social element and created benchmark scores for individuals to help drive motivation (or, in Stretchonomics terms, to keep runners 'hungry'). But the tracking app Strava has taken the art of (social) feedback to a new level; at the time of writing they are gaining a million new users every 45 days, capturing data from 161 million (bike) rides worldwide. The launch of Strava Metro, a private Twitter for users, has taken this social element to a new level for athletes of all descriptions. In effect, Strava have leveraged real-time feedback to create an entirely new social network – a perfect example of the herding instinct explored earlier in this book. What Strava are proving is that the desire to measure and compare in real time is a powerful way to drive our hunger, irrespective of our goal or playing field. It brings external and internal motivations together.

As an aside, fitness measurement is an area where the pivot principle can be seen in full effect. Players like Tom-Tom and Garmin, from the now largely redundant sat-nav market (remember when they weren't built into cars, or the likes of Waze or Google maps were not available on every phone?) are making big plays in sports watches and trackers – reusing and reapplying their GPS and mapping technologies on a smaller scale.

In sport, via the likes of Strava, and in our work lives, via the likes PD@GE, the feedback we get is broken down into two distinct types. We think of the first as 'Intrinsic Feedback'. Athletes and other individuals have in-built mechanisms telling them how well they have performed. They can *see* the results, can *sense* the movements that caused the results, and subconsciously they form perceptions about how they think they performed. Being able to visualise our performances like this allows us to form conclusions of our own. It drives a kind of self-improvement that comes from within, and this helps develop and sustain our intrinsic motivations.

'Augmented feedback', meanwhile, is the feedback that comes from elsewhere, whether that's another human being or a piece of technology recording what we do and how. Coaches might provide additional information or give athletes more detail about their performances, or the same function might be performed by a piece of technology. Having this additional data can help us narrow the gap between what we *think* we did and what actually happened, and, by interrogating this gap, we can identify ways to improve. In contrast to the above, this helps boost our extrinsic motivation.

Given the huge numbers of studies into the impact feedback – and in particular real time feedback – has on our motivation levels, it is perhaps not surprising to discover that measuring ourselves and receiving feedback helps manage our hunger. When students and athletes are given feedback on their performance, they not only value their performances more highly, they strive to improve as well. We don't always need it, but regular feedback can be invaluable when we're just embarking on a stretch, and it's useful, too (though perhaps needed less frequently) for athletes, executives and others already at the top of their game. Wherever you are in your stretch journey, the message is simple: if we're to perform at our highest we need to find ways of incorporating measurement and feedback into our daily schedules.

The Hunger Games

Our marathon runner has done it. He's staggered over the line, achieved his stretch ambition, and now he's sitting on the curb side covered in a space blanket trying to rehydrate, watching other runners coming in. Having got this far, having completed his first marathon, the first question he gets asked is, 'Would you do it again?' He knows that he has to do something. He has stretched and wants to challenge himself again… but how? At that moment, who knows?

1. Hunger is asking what comes next, even as you're accomplishing your first stretch goal.
2. Hunger is about managing the tension between where you are and where you're going. We call this the Two Chevron Principle.
3. We are all motivated by different things – both external (what others expect of us) and internal (what we expect of ourselves).
4. Internal motivation is more powerful and can drive real and lasting HUNGER.

5. Internal motivations are the oil that keeps our engine running, but external motivators can be the rockets that give us a sudden burst of performance.

6. There is often a lull after achieving a significant stretch goal. Deciding what's next and setting a new TARGET is the key to avoiding the Comfort Zone.

CONCLUSION

- We're all only as strong as our weakest link
- How to apply Stretchonomics to your own growth challenge.

Well, we're here. We've done it. We've explored each of the seven dimensions of Stretchonomics in detail. We've looked at our S, our T, our R, our E, T, C, and H – and along the way you may have spotted that no single aspect of Stretchonomics could exist without the other. It is an holistic model.

In our research and day-to-day work with start-ups and multinationals, working with those facing commercial growth challenges, it is clear to see that they are only as strong as their weakest link. The multinational looking to grow – which has a clear strategy and money to burn – which is let down by the final decisions of when and where to invest (COURAGE). The company hot on the heels of rapid growth that starts slipping backwards as they struggle to rediscover their hunger despite having the cash to invest (HUNGER). The start-up with the amazing tech and backers but lacking the true understanding of where and how to compete (SCOPE). The team leader stuck facing the same challenge as their predecessor but unable to see a way around repeating the mistakes of the past to generate new growth (EXECUTION or TECHNIQUES). The sports team with high aspirations but no money to invest in new players (RESOURCE). The cross-Pacific rowers looking to the next challenge (HUNGER) and how to reapply their skills (EXECUTION, TECHNIQUE). The guys who started to write a book 18 months ago with barely enough time to read a book, let alone write one

(RESOURCES), never having written one before (EXECUTION, TECHNIQUES). We have been through the Romer cycle, dealt with the Cougar in the Car... This book has been a Stretch journey in itself.

When gaps open up between an aspirational target and the behaviours and resources necessary to deliver it, a project can quickly unravel. Perhaps you fear your own journey is reaching this point now? If that's the case, it's time to submit to a Stretchonomics health-check. A Stretchonomics health-check isn't about maximising any one of these seven dimensions. It's about making sure that they're all in robust health, that they're all working in concert. Because if there is one thing fatal to the success of a Stretch, it's when there is an imbalance between ambition and the commitment (between the S & T and the others required to deliver it). Too much of one, too little of another and a Stretch can be undermined or an opportunity missed. We know this from both personal and professional experience

That's the very last of our Stretchonomics secrets: our chances of success are only as strong as our weakest link.

A Personal Story

Remember Albion Racing Club, our booze brand? Remember how we barrelled into the small batch craft spirits market when a client we were advising turned away from the opportunity? We did it in a spirit of adventure, with a passion for trying new things, and hoping, perhaps, that we might learn a little something about business, about ourselves and, of course, about whisky along the way. Our Albion adventure might have been a success in terms of how it has supported our consulting business with Mangrove – it provided us with a case study that demonstrated our skills, our accountability, our willingness to put our money where our mouth is, which both opened doors to new clients and reignited our relationships with old – but the cold hard truth is that it hasn't (yet) been a long-term commercial success.

Albion Racing Club taught us more about business, and more about Stretchonomics itself, than any of our other endeavours. It's still teaching us lessons today. But why didn't it 'succeed'? Where were our weak points? In seeking to understand why Albion Racing Club – or any of your own stretches – doesn't entirely succeed, a simple Stretchonomics diagnosis can be worthwhile, even if it is a little unpleasant (like broccoli or muesli). With a bit of ruthlessness and emotional detachment, we can all begin to pick apart our own endeavours and see the areas where, potentially, things began to go wrong. We have used Stretchonomics not only on our own business but with a range of multinationals and every time we learn something more about the model and those we are working with. We're even able to apply Stretchonomics principles to the writing of this *Stretchonomics* book itself...

Scope. Consulting is not a world that stays still for long, and we had reached a point where we needed to push our thinking beyond where we'd been for several years. We recognised that the world of innovation – and our view of it – had changed, becoming less about finding the silver bullet ideas that could transform a life, and more about working hard to find opportunities for growth, and to make average ideas great by nurturing them over time. However, not everyone we worked with appreciated the scale of these changes, nor their implications, and, what's more, we were ourselves struggling to articulate how what we offered our consulting clients had changed. We had to find a way of describing our new, more holistic view of how to achieve growth. Whatever that was, we knew it had to not only speak to our current clients but broaden our audience as well. We wanted to capture much of what we'd learned over the years and bring it all together in a cohesive piece of thinking. Perhaps, we began to think, writing a book was the best step forward?

Target. Once we'd settled on the idea to write a book, we knew we would need it to (a) appeal to a publisher; (b) be on a par with other books we admire – many referenced in this book; and (c) be researched, written and published within twelve months. This was a bold and stretching target for two people who had not only never written a book before, but who also had busy day jobs and family lives. Yet we resolved that this was the right target for us, and our view was that, if it was worth doing at all, we should do it properly. After all, we were only going to ever write one book – so it had better be a good one.

Resource. We knew from the outset that the resource most likely to challenge or restrict our ambition (S&T) would be time. And this was exactly what happened as we set about our stretch. From the beginning, everything took longer than planned – developing the overall idea, creating a structure, researching each chapter... and, of course, writing the damn thing. We quickly realised that we needed to adjust part of our T, and, given that we weren't going to compromise on quality, we had to give ourselves more time and delay the publishing date.

Execution. Once we had the outline of the idea, we needed to develop and refine it. This was not as easy a process as we had anticipated. First off, we had to find a name for our theory, something that could also become the snappy title of our book. Next, we needed to break our thinking down into the seven dimensions about which you've just read. And this was only the beginning of the work it took to put this book together. We had to lay out the chapter plan, for the publisher as well as for ourselves. We had to conduct interviews, do the research and then begin to do the most frightening thing of all: put words on a page. Rightly or wrongly, we approached it in the same way we would a consulting job, and sought early and regular feedback from our publisher to ensure we were on track.

Techniques. Despite this being our first book, the skills we had acquired through our day jobs gave us a head start: synthesising lots of information into something digestible, making complex concepts simple and accessible, and conducting desk research and interviews, were all things we were used to doing with *Mangrove*. We were well equipped to tackle these tasks, but the one area in which we lacked experience and capability was the writing itself. This was our skills gap and, given our lack of time, the best way to bridge it was to employ the help of a talented freelance writer and editor (thanks Rob!)

Courage. Our Big C was taking the decision to write a book in the first place. And believe us, we have certainly hit the inevitable roadblocks along the way – so there have been many opportunities to exercise our Little C as well. For us, the risks of not finishing this stretch were minimal – the only real risk was damage to our reputations. Yet we were well aware that there was a danger we would slip back into the Comfort Zone if we didn't constantly force ourselves to find a way to make it work. It took a long time, but we got there. Two years after we embarked upon this stretch, we limped across the finish line, and there's no doubt that our resilience has been thoroughly tested along the way. This project has pushed us through Romner's six stages (awesome, tricky, this is shit, I am shit, this might be ok, back to awesome) without mercy.

Hunger. It would have been easy to give up at any stage along the journey, but our motivations for doing this were internal and therefore deeply seated. To maintain our motivation we regularly shared progress with trusted confidants – from the initial idea through each draft chapter. It was the positive feedback we received along the way that kept us going. During the process, we also put our thinking to the test with clients and partners in real life situations, and the results of these 'trials' helped us stay within two chevrons of the goal. This real-time feedback has been invaluable in pushing us to produce something of which we are incredibly proud. Who knows whether the next challenge will be another start-up, a whisky brand or another book… but it won't be long before we will be starting something new and going through the cycle again.

We've said all along that anyone embarking upon a new stretch – whether that's individually or as a business – is only as strong as their weakest links. For us, these were our Resources and Techniques. To be brutal: we didn't have enough time (R) to write the book, not alongside all our other work and personal commitments; and nor, we soon realised, did we have the ability to write in a structured yet compelling way (T). Once we'd diagnosed where our weaknesses were, we were able to go out and remedy them – something that, serendipitously, wouldn't have been possible without the principles of *Stretchonomics* itself.

The Five Tips

To achieve success (however we define it) we need, above all else, to stay in our Stretch Zones. When one of our Stretchonomics dimensions begins to wax or wane, it's time to look at ourselves and review where we're going. Are we at risk of slipping out of the Stretch Zone? Why are we slipping and in which direction? How are we faring on all seven dimensions of Stretch?

Fortunately, the Stretchonomics framework allows us the tools to do exactly this. It's an early warning system designed to identify threats before they have an impact on performance. If your HUNGER isn't right, find out about it early and find new ways to motivate. If your COURAGE has been faltering, well, get out there and start flexing those Little C COURAGE muscles. And, if your RESOURCES are under pressure, look back at your SCOPE and TARGET and adjust them accordingly.

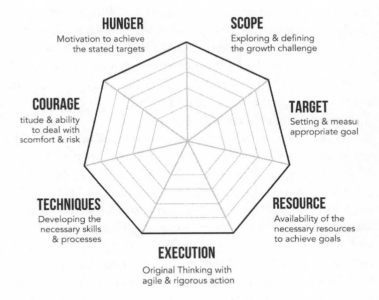

HUNGER
Motivation to achieve
the stated targets

SCOPE
Exploring & defining
the growth challenge

COURAGE
titude & ability
to deal with
scomfort & risk

TARGET
Setting & measu
appropriate goal

TECHNIQUES
Developing the
necessary skills
& processes

RESOURCE
Availability of the
necessary resources
to achieve goals

EXECUTION
Original Thinking with
agile & rigorous action

Treat Stretchonomics as a way to both diagnose and treat your stretches. Its principles can be applied to anyone in any situation that involves lifting yourself up out of the Comfort Zone:

1. Always Begin With Ambition (S-T)

Understand your motivations and explore the full range of opportunities in front of you, in order to set a realistic target. Don't ever be embarrassed by setting a modest target. If that's what your resources and hunger dictate, then embrace it! Over-ambition is as dangerous as no ambition at all. Set your S and T well – and only then explore what's required of you in terms of R, E, T, C and H.

2. Commit (R-E-T-C-H)

To stay successfully in the Stretch Zone, your commitments are going to have to match your ambitions. But be honest about what commitments you have. What resources are available to you? (Remember that time, energy and emotion are resources in just the same way as money and raw materials). What techniques do you have? How are you flexing your courage muscles, and how are you managing your hunger? Your R, E, T, C and H can all be practised and stretched in their own ways, but they have to work in alignment with your S and T – so don't be afraid to revisit and tweak them, if your commitments demand it.

3. Understand Your Weakest Dimensions

To maximise your chances of success, be clear and honest from the very beginning about which Stretch dimensions are most likely to let you down. If you know your COURAGE is going to be lacking, or your RESOURCES are tight, or that you don't have as full a range of TECHNIQUES as you might need, you can plan to mitigate the risk. This might mean looking again at your SCOPE and TARGET, or it might be by working to boost your commitment to the particular stretch. Don't be afraid of seeking help from others. Address those weaknesses however works best for you. Remember the benefits of the growth mind-set: courage, hunger, confidence, creativity – these are all traits we can acquire by practising them, in exactly the same way as a body builder develops his body.

4. Adapt and React To Stay In the Stretch Zone

If you're venturing into the Stretch Zone for the first time, accept that what worked for you in the Comfort Zone won't be enough to succeed in the more challenging arena of Stretch. That's why you came here – embrace it! Once you're in the Stretch Zone, beware your biggest enemy. Complacency can be a killer, or at the very least can compromise any aspirations. Don't assume that what got you into the Stretch Zone is going to keep you in the Stretch Zone. Chances are, you'll need to adapt and improve over time in order to stay there. Examine your Stretch dimensions regularly and be honest about how each is faring. Be prepared to adjust your SCOPE and TARGET, to set new goals and ambitions. Develop response strategies that you can employ every time you feel the pull of the

Comfort Zone, or a new Comfort Zone crystallising around you. This may all seem uncomfortable now, but take that as a positive sign – no pain, no gain!

5. Use The Comfort Zone Wisely

You've come this far. You don't need reminding that the Comfort Zone isn't conducive to growth. But we all have to retreat there at times. There might be times, in business and life, when the Comfort Zone can be used as a tool. Use it wisely. After sustained periods of effort, it's only natural to pause and catch one's breath, before returning to the fray once again. A short spell of respite can be a good thing. Just remember that the Comfort Zone has an allure that it can be hard to escape. Be vigilant and develop the ability to recognise when you've been there too long: the feeling of being *too* comfortable, the loss of uncertainty, being unable to remember how it felt when you last got out there and did something new, the adrenaline rushing through your veins. When we're not going forwards, we're in danger of slipping back. If you've been in the Comfort Zone too long, make plans to get out there and continue your journey. It may require a few more tweaks to some of your Stretch dimensions but, in the end, the rewards will be worth it.

One Last Stretch

The Stretch Zone is not just accessible to the extraordinary. And nor is Stretchonomics. That's the beauty of the model, whether your goal is to be the first four-person team of women rowers to cross the Pacific Ocean, to launch a new business, or run a marathon. Across the last decade we have worked with elite sports teams, multinational corporations, start-ups and all manner of other organisations, and we believe that – whether you're seasoned or start-up – the core concepts of Stretchonomics are just as pertinent for us all.

It works. It works for the individual. It works for the business looking to reorient itself or simply to just grow. It worked for us and we hope it will work for you. We've shared our stories with you, what we've learned from our day jobs, research and side-ventures – and, whatever your Stretch ambition, whether you succeed or fail, we'd love to hear yours.

In this book we have tried to make our ideas as accessible as possible. We feel that although the ideas have come from our professional lives they are equally relevant to the 'real' world. In writing the book we have necessarily had to gloss over many of the details of how these concepts work in businesses and how we apply them in order to positively impact business growth and performance. We have shied away from the Techniques and Executional details. We felt that would be another book entirely – one with narrower appeal that would be a tougher read. However, should you want to know more about the application of Stretchonomics to businesses large or small please do visit us at www.stretchonomics.co.uk or email us at stretch@mangroveconsulting.co.uk or on Twitter at @stretchonomics.

ACKNOWLEDGEMENTS

This book is the culmination of everything we have learned in our careers to date. We're fortunate to have worked with some smart people, on some amazing brands and in a variety of great businesses. Every project has been a learning experience and we are grateful for the opportunities that have stretched us and fuelled the thinking in this book. We've met some incredible individuals along the way, many of whom are mentioned or alluded to in these pages. They have impacted us more than they might know.

Huge thanks go to Robert Dinsdale, our talented and patient editor who help filled the blanks and turn our often rambling thoughts into readable prose, and to Humfrey at Silvertail Books who bought the concept on the basis of our extremely amateurish pitch.

And finally, we would like to thank our families. Living with someone going through a "Stretch" is not always easy, and we're aware that filling our houses with booze and books, making moonshine in the kitchen, and the disruptive late night and early morning editing have been trying. So, apologies, and thanks for putting up with us.

NOTES

1. 'Drive: The Surprising Truth About What Motivates Us', Daniel Pink (2009)
2. State of the American Manager: Analytics and Advice for Leaders (Gallup, 2015)
3. Eason Ding and Tim Hursery, University of Oregon Department of Economics, 2016.
4. 'Reduced Specificity of Personal Goals and Explanations for Goal Attainment in Major Depression' by Joanne M. Dickson and Nicholas J. Moberly, PLOS One.
5. 'Hijacked By Your Brain' by Dr Julian Ford and Jon Wortmann, Sourcebooks (2012)
6. Anna Kegler, psychology journalist at the *Huffington Post*
7. Carole Dweck, *Mindset*, 2006
8. 'The top-down influence of ergogenic placebos on muscle work and fatigue', European Journal of Neuroscience, July 2008
9. http://www.trainingscience.net/?page_id=128
10. 'Strategy as Stretch Leverage' by Coimbatore Prahalad, the late professor of corporate strategy at the University of Michigan and Dr Gary Hamel, American management expert; Harvard Business Review, 1993
11. Kushlev and Dunn, Computers in Human Behaviour, Vol 43, Feb 2015
12. The Enchanted World of Sleep, Peretz Lavie (University of Yale Press)
13. Gillian Tett, THE SILO EFFECT, (Little Brown, 2015)

14. Harris Interactive online survey on behalf of CareerBuilder, 2013.

15. Shane Snow, co-founder and Chief Creative Officer of Contently.

16. Drew Boyd, assistant professor of marketing and innovation at the University of Cincinnati; Jacob Goldenberg, professor of marketing at the Hebrew University of Jerusalem's School of Business Administration.

17. The International Centre for Studies in Creativity at Buffalo College in New York

18. Matthew Syed, *Bounce*

19. Daniel Coyle, *The Talent Code*; Geoff Colvin, Talent is Overrated

20. 2015 study by Deloitte's, *Becoming Irresistible*.

CPSIA information can be obtained
at www.ICGtesting.com
Printed in the USA
BVHW03s1230040418
512448BV00008B/738/P